Campaign Planner

for INTEGRATED BRAND COMMUNICATIONS

3 E

Frisby
scPrinciples (54700)

SHAY SAYRE

California State University, Fullerton

THOMSON

SOUTH-WESTERN

Australia · Canada · Mexico · Singapore · Spain · United Kingdom · United States

THOMSON

SOUTH-WESTERN

Campaign Planner for Integrated Brand Communications, 3e

Shay Sayre

VP/Editorial Director:
Jack W. Calhoun

VP/Editor-in-Chief:
Dave Shaut

Senior Publisher:
Melissa S. Acuña

Executive Editor:
Neil Marquardt

Sr. Developmental Editor:
Mardell Toomey

Marketing Manager:
Nicole C. Moore

Production Editor:
Emily S. Gross

Sr. Manufacturing Coordinator:
Diane Lohman

Art Director:
Stacy Jenkins Shirley

Production House:
OffCenter Concept House

Cover Designer:
Nick Gliebe/Design Matters
Cincinnati, OH

Cover Image:
© Getty Images, Inc.

Printer:
West Group
Eagan, MN

For permission to use material
from this text or product, submit a
request online at
http://www.thomsonrights.com.
Any additional questions about
permissions can be submitted by
email to
thomsonrights@thomson.com.

For more information
contact South-Western,
5191 Natorp Boulevard,
Mason, Ohio, 45040.
Or you can visit our Internet site
at: http://www.swlearning.com

Campaign Planner
for
Integrated Brand Communications

TABLE OF CONTENTS

Section I What We're Doing
  A. Why We Use the Campaign Planner   2
  B. How We Use This Planner   3
  C. What Is a Campaign?   4

Section II Choose Your Client and Staff Your Agency
  A. Pick a Brand, Any Brand   8
    1. Monster Energy Drink   9
    2. Calloway Golf Equipment   11
    3. Public Broadcast System   12
    4. Napster Online Music   15
    5. Your Local Business or Service   17
  B. What Job Do You Want?   18
    1. Agency Roles   18
    2. Agency Rules   19
    3. Your Profile and Agency Preference   21
  C. Developing Agency Relationships: Team-Building Activities   22

Section III Keeping Track: Agency Meeting Rosters
  A. Agency Meeting Rosters   24
    1. Meeting 1: Organize your agency   25
    2. Meeting 2: Prepare the   26
    3. Meeting 3: Complete the situation analysis   27
    4. Meeting 4: Identify audience segment and competition   28
    5. Meeting 5: Allocate the budget and position the brand   29
    6. Meeting 6: Set communication objectives and brand message   30
    7. Meeting 7: Determine creative strategies   31
    8. Meeting 8: Set media objectives   32
    9. Meeting 9: Create promotional activities   33
    10. Meeting 10: Establish evaluation criteria and choose presenters   35
    11. Meeting 11: Assemble plans book and rehearse presentation   36
    12. Meeting 12: Rehearse the presentation and evaluate your efforts   37
  B. Agency Evaluation and Final Report   38

Section IV Ten Steps to Building a Great Campaign Plan
  A. It's the Planning, Stupid!   40
    1. Step 1: Conduct the Situation Analysis   41
    2. Step 2: Profile the Consumer Segment   47

3.   Step 3. Analyze the Competition   51

4.   Step 4: Allocate the Budget   53

5.   Step 5: Establish a Brand Positioning Strategy   54

6.   Step 6: Determine the Communication Objectives and Advertising Message   56

7.   Step 7: Develop the Creative Strategy   58

8.   Step 8: Set Media Objectives and Strategies   61

9.   Step 9: Create Rewarding Promotions   63

10.   Step 10: Set Evaluation Criteria   66

Section V Campaign Aids and Activities

A. Research Aids   68

    1. Web sites   68

    2. Survey instruments   70

    3. Survey tally sheet   76

B. Helpful Hints   77

    1. Tips for Planning an Event   77

    2. Tips for Selecting Sponsorships and Partnerships   78

    3. Tips for Writing a News Release   79

C. How to Ask for the Order: The Art of Presenting   80

    1. Why we present and who we present to   80

    2. Use your memory or PowerPoint   80

    3. Use an easy-to-follow format   81

    4. Some of the best ways to open   81

    5. Overall   82

    6. To avoid surprises, always rehearse   82

    7. Must-do rules for success   82

D. Xtracredit Assignment   83

    1. Information Interview   83

    2. Books to Read   86

Section VI Preparing the Plans Book

A. Putting It All Together: Preparing the Plans Books   90

B. Student Example: Toni&Guy Plans Book   91

    I.   SITUATION ANALYSIS

        A. Personal Care Industry   93

        B. Company & Brand History   93

        C. Product Evaluation   100

        D. Competitive Analysis   100

        E. Consumer Evaluation   104

    II.   SWOT ANALYSIS   107

    III.   GOALS & OBJECTIVES

        A. Marketing Objectives   111

        B. Communications Objectives   111

    IV.   BUDGET   112

    V.   CREATIVE BRIEF   115

    VI.   MEDIA PLAN

        A. Media Objectives   121

    B. Media Strategy   122
  VII. SALES PROMOTION RECOMMENDATIONS   124
 VIII. PUBLIC RELATIONS RECOMMENDATIONS   126
  IX. DATABASE MARKETING RECOMMENDATIONS 126
   X. CAMPAIGN EVALUATION   127
   XI. REFERENCES   128

SECTION I
What We're Doing

Why We Use the Campaign Planner

This workbook is designed to help you prepare a campaign in conjunction with principles texts in advertising, promotion, brand, or Integrated Marketing Communications. To produce the campaign, you may work alone or in agency teams. By combining the information in your text with the ten-step program included in this Planner, you will be able to successfully design and present a professional campaign.

Perfect for Instructors. Student team leaders collect assignments, take attendance and evaluate member participation in both small and large classes. By placing responsibility for administration of group activity on the students, instructors are free to concentrate on advising and avoiding the cumbersome tracking activity usually associated with team supervision.

Perfect for Students. These step-by-step instructions guide students both individually and as a team to develop a fool-proof Plans Book and effective campaign. Everything you need is here—surveys, examples and helpful hints—just follow the easy directions in each section of the Planner.

How We Use This Planner

The planner is divided into six sections. Here's why.

Section I explains how the Planner works and introduces you to TiGi and Bed Head, our brand example.

Section II profiles four brands from which you will choose your campaign client. Or you may prefer to select the local business or service option instead. When teams are formed, you will select an agency role for this campaign. To get your agency ready to work together, try one of the team-building activities provided here.

Section III contains rosters for 12 agency meetings and an agency evaluation form. Meeting rosters provide direction for gathering information and making decisions necessary for developing your campaign.

Section IV presents a 10–Step guide with planning and execution activities. These steps provide all the information necessary for writing a campaign Plans Book. Each planning activity is completed prior to the agency meeting with a corresponding number – Step Two prior to Meeting 2.

Section V includes aids to help with campaign research, executions and presentation. Extra credit assignments are also included.

Section VI provides instructions on how to assemble a Plans Book. A sample PowerPoint presentation and a sample student campaign Plans Book are also included.

But before we begin, let's define "campaign" and orient you to the task at hand.

What Is a Campaign?

A Campaign is the sum of its parts...

A campaign has many parts: **Advertisements** are part of a campaign. Editorial features that come from **public relations** efforts are part of a campaign. Sponsorships, special events, licensed merchandise, direct mail, Web sites—all of these **promotional elements** are part of a campaign. Because no single commercial, feature story, or promotion can create the necessary brand awareness for a product or service, an effective **integration** of all brand communication elements is essential for a successful campaign.

So, our working definition of campaign is:
> *A themed series of **coordinated brand messages** delivered to a specific **target audience** through a variety of **promotional media & activities** during a fixed **period of time**.*

Take a look at the components of this definition.

Coordinated brand messages are presented in various forms, including:
- Paid advertisements for space and/or time
- Brand appearances or mentions in TV sitcoms, books and movies
- Logos that adorn clothing and sporting goods
- Corporate associations with charitable organizations
- Coupons redeemable at retail outlets
- Themed amusements or restaurants
- Sporting events and entertainment venues
- Feature stories in all forms of media
- Neon signs, Web banners, and spinnaker sails
- Hood ornaments, celebrities and fruit stickers
- Blimps, NASCAR vehicles, and popular art

- Murals, comic books and pets
- And so on and so on

Target audiences consist of consumer aggregates:
- current brand/product users
- potential brand/product users
- users of the competition's brand/product

Promotional media and activities include:
- Print
- Broadcast
- Internet
- New Media
- Sponsorships
- Events
- Product placement
- Incentives

Campaign time limits usually extend from six months to several years. Some brands change the creative executions of their campaigns regularly. Coke and Pepsi constantly rotate singing stars and animated creatures to promote their brands. Absolut Vodka and Maytag Appliances are examples of successful long-running campaigns. Absolut has featured its distinctive bottle and Maytag the lonely repairman since both company's mediated messages began decades ago.

online Take a closer look at some memorable campaigns as presented by *Advertising Age* magazine at their Web site, http://www.adage.com/century/campaigns.html
Or view a portfolio of problems and campaign solutions at http://www.landor.com/portfolio
Or view a public service campaign at http://www.energyexperts.areva.com/areva_us.html

SECTION II
Choose Your Client And Staff Your Agency

Who do we work for and what do we do?

Pick a Brand, Any Brand

National and Global Brands

You or your agency may select from the four brands included in this section. Three of the brands are publicly held companies with global distribution; the fourth is a media service. After reading each company's synopsis, select the brand best suited to your interest and experience. Web sites are provided for in-depth background information. These case profiles are offered in abbreviated form and are in no way intended to be considered complete.

Local Focus

If you or your instructor prefer your agency to develop a campaign for a local business, consult available resources to develop a brief synopsis of the company on your own. Contact your local Chamber of Commerce or go to http://www.digitalcity.com for regional assistance.

You may also want to consult the nearest advertising association for campaign suggestions. For a great resource to local advertising clubs in most US cities, a university ad club, or advertising associations worldwide, go to http://utexas.edu/coc/adv/world/AW300.html.

Pick from these clients:

Monster Energy

Calloway Golf Company

PUBLIC BROADCASTING SERVICE

Napster Online Music

Monster Energy

http://www.monsterenergy.com   Nasdaq: HANS

The Energy Drink Industry
Red Bull founded the energy drink product category in 1997. In 2003, energy drinks dominated the specialty beverage category of the beverage industry. Mainly teas and juices mixed with herbal, vitamin, and mineral supplements, the energy drink segment accounted for $20 billion dollars, about one fifth of revenues from the specialty beverage category. Energy drinks have been backed up by some heavy duty marketing spending in recent years, offering benefits ranging from giving consumers "fast alertness" to providing them with "wings"'.

Company Background
Hansen's Natural Corporation, developer of Monster Energy Drink, is a longtime maker of natural sodas and juices since 1935 and producer of many avant-guarde drinks targeted toward affluent, health-conscious, high achieving consumers. Hansen's has created two drink categories to cover a wide variety of beverage consumers: energy drinks and health beverages. Recognized nationally, Hansen's is a label with products named not for their flavor but for what they can do for the consumer.

Rodney Sacks, current chairman and CEO, bought Hansen's Natural Corporation with a group of investors in 1992 from California Company Packers Corporation, a Hawaiian company that had purchased Hansen's assets through federal bankruptcy court. Headquartered in Anaheim, California, Hansen's faces competition from a myriad of newcomers involved in the energy drink market.

Target Market
Health-conscious, young professionals and students 16–34 years of age prefer this "New Age beverage" because it exudes a hip and edgy vibe that reflects their lifestyles. Professional athletes and sports participants also use energy drinks to enhance their performance. Anyone who needs to stay alert—long-distance drivers, salesmen, police—is considered a potential user of the product. Clubbers are known to mix energy drinks with vodka for a night on the town.

Marketing Mix

Product
Performance enhancers and exotic ingredients create classic buzz staples—-caffeine and sugar—that promise a powerful energy boost. Energy drinks

have about four times as much caffeine as colas, and their sugar levels are also much higher than average soft drinks. It comes in a 16-ounce can.

Place
Monster Energy is mass-marketed to convenience stores and chain grocery stores. Monster cases are available in club stores in the U.S. and Canada. Online wholesale orders are competitively priced.

Price
Prices vary; a multi-pack case of 24 sixteen-ounce cans retails for about $60 and wholesales for $40.

Promotion
Monster sponsors motocross riders and events around North America. A Monster's music contest selected twenty unsigned garage musicians to present their music online where visitors to the site could play Flash-based music and rate the winning songs. "Monster Mixers" are hosted at clubs around the country. Hansens, the parent company, contributes to the City of Hope Breast Cancer Research Center; consumers send in red tabs from cans to stimulate donations.

Brand Characteristics
- *Brand image:* The product's name and aggressive design, communicating a "bad boy" image, are in tune with its core consumers.
- *Brand personality*: Monster is mean, cool, mysterious, sinister, cute and fun. The brand has an attitude that invites drinkers to "unleash the beast!"
- *Brand equity*: Has the right ingredients to deliver an energy buzz. Has value—more product for the same price. Great tasting and fast acting in a super-sized can. Unique green graphic and logo.

Problem
Monster Energy must compete with the segment leader, Red Bull, as well as 30 other energy drink products. With an established market where the top five brands have 89% of the market share, Hansen's must develop innovative strategies to differentiate the drink from others, and do so with a much smaller budget than its corporate competitors.

Campaign Objective
Position Monster Energy as the product that delivers image, personality, effectiveness, taste, and value to consumer. Create an attitude that sets Monster apart from Red Bull in the minds of energy drinkers.

Calloway Golf Company

http://www.calloway.com   NYSE: ELY

Industry Overview
Golf is one of the most widely enjoyed leisure pastimes in America. In 2000, 26.7 million golfers played on 17,000 courses nationwide. Since 2000, the number of golfers has been steadily declining to its 2004 low, decreasing 5.2% in the number of rounds played annually. An economic downturn and job layoffs are blamed for the slowdown in purchases of golf equipment. The industry, however, remains the leader in consumer spending in the sporting goods equipment segment, with golf equipment sales at $3.7 billion, even in a stagnant market.

Company Background
Originally named Hickory Stick USA, Inc., the company was founded in Temecula California in 1982 by Ely Callaway. The company is publicly held and employs more than 2500 men and women worldwide. Their Carlsbad facility has a state-of-the-art testing center responsible for new technology development using aerospace applications. Their mission is to create superior equipment for golfers at all skill levels.

Target Market
College educated men and women 31-64 years old at all playing levels with incomes above $70,000. Because of the link between golf and business, many players are executives in managerial positions who take their clients out for a game of golf. College golfers are a secondary target segment.

Marketing Mix

Products
Clubs: metal woods, irons, woods and putters; golf balls: HX Blue and Red brands; and accessories: golf bags, gloves, headwear, travel covers, towels, and umbrellas make up the product lines. Calloway is best known for its Big Bertha Woods line of oversized titanium clubs.

11

Place
Callaway is a global company conducting business in 107 countries. Products are sold by authorized retailers, including large sports equipment chains and small pro shops.

Price
Callaway products are considered premium, tending to be priced higher than competitors. Clubs retail between $159 and $599 each.

Promotion
Sponsors individual golfers and the annual U.S. Woman's Open. Uses celebrity endorsements in print and television advertising. Calloway Golf Foundation has made $5 million in grants to charities.

Brand Characteristics
- *Brand image*: New production and innovative products marketed to all levels of players; caters to the average golfer's needs.
- *Brand personality:* Reliable, high energy and trustworthy.
- *Brand equity:* Big Bertha Woods, top-of-mind brand recognition, two year written warranty on clubs, industry awards for "best driver" and "best of the best" in golf clubs. Callaway Golf Training Organization among nation's best golf schools.

Problem
Declining sales, limited number of suppliers, inability to meet international demands, and devaluations of foreign currencies relative to the U.S. dollar put Callaway at a competitive disadvantage with Nike and Taylor Made (Adidas owned). These and other competitors have contributed to the decrease in brand equity for Callaway.

Campaign Objective
Re-establish Callaway as a premium brand and industry leader by targeting new and emerging golfers with technologically superior products.

PUBLIC BROADCASTING SERVICE
http://www.pbs.org

Industry Overview
Most broadcast companies are privately owned and provide programming on network television stations funded by either advertising or paid subscription services sold through cable and satellite companies. Only one broadcast service operates as a nonprofit enterprise, funded solely by donations from members, individual donors, corporations and/or foundations.

Company Background
Founded in 1969, the Public Broadcasting Service (PBS) is a private, nonprofit corporation whose members are America's public TV stations. PBS oversees program acquisition, distribution and promotion; educational services; new media ventures; fundraising support; engineering and technology development; and video marketing. There are 170 noncommercial educational licensees operating 349 PBS member stations. Licensees include 87 community organizations, 57 colleges or universities, twenty state authorities, and six local educational or municipal authorities.

Target Market
Public television audiences reflect the social and economic makeup of the nation. Seventy-one percent of all American television-owning families (75.7 million households representing 143.6 million people) watched PBS in October 2002, with the average home tuning in for over 7 1/2 hours during the month.

Marketing Mix

Product
PBS provides educational services, programming activities and companion Web sites to its audiences.
1. *Educational service*—Ready to Learn helps to increase school readiness through children's programming, books, magazines, parent workshops, and other learning resources. Adult Learning provides college credit TV courses.
2. *Programming activities*—programs feature children's, cultural, educational, history, nature, news, public affairs, science, and skills programs that are obtained from PBS stations, independent producers, and sources around the world. PBS does not produce programming.
3. *Digital leadership*—PBS.org is the most-visited dot-org Web site in the world, providing companion Web sites for more than 500 PBS TV programs and specials, plus original Web content and real-time learning adventures. It has groundbreaking work in interactive TV and a monthly

schedule of original high-definition programming to both the PBS KIDS Channel and PBS YOU multicast services.

Place
Provides television programming and relatged services to 349 noncommercial stations serving all 50 states, Puerto Rico, the U.S. Virgin Islands, Guam and American Samoa.

Price
Programs are free. Revenue is generated from members (23.5%), state governments (18.3%), Corporation for Public Broadcasting and federal grants/ contracts (16.4%), businesses (16.1%), state colleges and universities (6.5%), and foundations (5.5%).

Promotion
Part of the revenue generated is spent on advertising and the promotion of programming activities and schedules.

Brand Characteristics
- *Brand image:* educational, reliable, trustworthy, accurate
- *Brand personality*: introverted, serious (young adults) and playful (children/parents)
- *Brand equity*: Award-winning news, documentary and children's programming; Web site; educational activities; logo; membership loyalty.

Problem
Many PBS services go unnoticed and unused because of a lack of information about programs and other offerings. Although children's programs have a high awareness level from parents, teachers, and youngsters, teens and young adult audiences remain unaware of PBS entertainment offerings.

Campaign Objective
Develop a campaign using advertising and promotions that generates program awareness with young adults (19–24) and teens (14–18) through print and broadcast media. Reverse the attitude that PBS is purely educational with no entertainment value for young adults.

Napster Online Music

http://www.napster.com   Nasdaq: ROXI

Industry Overview
Until 2003, the online music business has been plagued by piracy, illegal file sharing, and copyright infringement lawsuits. In the first three months of 2004, however, 25 million digital tracks were sold. The rise of paid online services and growing popularity of portable digital music players signals an even greater demand for digital music in this critical early-growth stage.

Company Background
Owned by Roxio Digital Media Company, Napster is the world's most recognized brand for downloading music tracks and transferring songs to portable devices, or burning them to CDs. It is the first PC-only digital music service to sell over five million downloads. In its first year of operation under its Santa Clara, California ownership, Napster is expected to generate at least $20 million in revenues.

Target Market
Music lovers ages 12-35 who own computers and/or portable DMPs.

Marketing Mix

Product
Online music store for song downloads; digital music access for university students. Has 1/2 million songs and a free online magazine. Subscription services include unlimited downloading, billboard charts, song clips, 50 free commercial radio stations, and a collection of interactive play lists.

Price
As of April, 2004, album prices are $13.99, and singles are $.99.

Place
Downloads from the Internet site; prepaid Napster download cards available in over 26,000 retail locations.

Promotion
Advertising and online presence.

Brand Characteristics
- *Brand image:* Hip, funky and "out- there."
- *Brand personality*: Takes its personality from the trademarked cat character that conveys playfulness.

- *Brand equity*: New ownership, name recognition, recording artist selection.

Problem

A rash of new services offering music for subscription, download, or both and Apple's iTunes Music Store pose a serious threat to Napster's leadership position.

Campaign Objective

Convince new and current users of digital music services that Napster has more advantages and better service than the competition.

Local Business or Service

Industry Overview
Using business periodicals and Internet sites, analyze trends in your client's industry.

Company Background
You will develop a company profile from brochures, Web sites or other information that will expand the actual campaign. Identify competitors.

Target Market
Identify the current users and potential customers of this business and profile them.

Marketing Mix

Product
Describe the product(s) or service and its features and benefits. Be prepared to evaluate their strengths and weaknesses.

Place
Identify where the business is located and how it distributes its product or service.

Price
Discuss the pricing strategy as well as actual prices.

Promotion
Outline all the current advertising, promotion, public relations, sponsorships, Web sites, etc. that are currently being used by the business or service. Try to determine the approximate amount of their budget.

Brand Characteristics
- *Brand image* – how is the brand perceived by consumers?
- *Brand character* – what is the brand's personality?
- *Brand equity* – what strengths and attributes does the brand possess?

Problem
You have one of two choices here: 1) describe a problem you can identify as existing, or 2) ask your contact at the business what problems they are having with promotion. Define the problem as a communication objective, such as "lack of awareness" or "bad brand image".

Campaign Objective
The objective corresponds directly to the problem. If the problem is lack of awareness, then the campaign objective is to create or increase awareness. If the brand image is poor, the campaign will improve or change consumer attitudes about it. Don't try to re-design the product, just deal with problems that can be solved through advertising, promotion and/or IBC strategies and tactics.

What Job Do You Want?

First, read the chapter in your text about advertising agency roles.

Next, review each of the agency positions presented in this section and select the one that is closest to what you would like to do when you graduate, or one that capitalizes on a talent you already have.
If you cannot decide, select the account planning position, which offers an opportunity to be an advocate for consumers in agency decisions.

Agency Roles

Account Executive
As an AE, you assume the greatest responsibility for the agency's performance. You assign tasks, make certain that deadlines are met, and are responsible for assembling the final Plans Book. You evaluate agency members' performance and make final determinations when disputes or problems occur. *Take this job if you have the time, energy and commitment to run an agency.*

Account Manager
As a manager, you assist the AE and assume that role when the AE is absent. You keep all written records and act as the recorder for attendance and activities of agency members. You are also responsible for keeping track of deadlines and making certain that tasks are completed properly. *Take this job if you are organized, efficient, and can work well with the AE.*

Account Planner
Account planners conduct research on behalf of the consumer. They find out what consumers want and expect from a brand, and how they perceive the brand's image. APs are responsible for collecting surveys, analyzing results and preparing a research report for the Plans Book. *This important job is ideal for people who enjoy developing creative ways to both gather consumer opinions and interpret their wishes in order for the creative team to develop a copy platform.*

Media Planner
Planners make recommendations for tactics once the media strategy has been decided. For instance, if your team decides to use Web banner advertising, you would decide on which sites the banner would be placed. You also prepare a media schedule and make budget allocations for media placements. *If you have a head for figures, this is the job for you.*

Creative Team—Art Director
The art director develops creative concepts and executions for advertisements and Web pages. You work with the writer to prepare ad

executions. *If you have both artistic talent and skills in computer graphics, take this job.*

Creative Team—Copywriter

Copywriters compose headlines, copy for print ads, and writes scripts and storyboards for electronic media. You work with the artist to prepare ad executions. *If you have a talent for writing, take this job.*

Sales Promotions Director

The director of promotions creates retail and consumer sales promotions for the brand to induce trial and increase usage. *If you like to develop incentives to stimulate purchases, this job is for you.*

Public Relations Director

The PR director decides how to reach consumers through non-paid placements in all forms of media, and picks a philanthropic organization to help the company maintain a positive image. You write a news release and suggest feature ideas for the brand. You develop sponsorship opportunities and plan special events. *If you enjoy the challenge of getting free media coverage and developing special events and sponsorship opportunities, you'll like this job.*

Production Director

The production director is the person responsible for putting together the Plans Book, creating PowerPoint presentations, and producing the Plans Book for your client and instructor. *If you're good at graphics and layout, you'll want this job.*

AGENCY RULES

Working together as a team requires operational rules to which everyone must agree. As a member of this agency, your participation and cooperation is important to the team's success—and grade! Please read these rules and sign the Profile and Preferences form to confirm your agreement with them.

1. Members must
   - complete the assigned Planning Step before attending agency meetings
   - attend all agency meetings; in case of illness, send your Planning sheet to the AE via e-mail
   - be responsible and complete your job requirements on time

2. Agencies have the right
   - to fire a team member for assignment delinquency and/or frequent absenteeism. The delinquent or absent member receives one week's warning to reverse his/her behavior. If the problem persists, a unanimous vote by agency members will eliminate that member from the team.

3. Account executive has the power to make a final decision
   - on an agency-related issue
   - member delinquency and/or termination
   - member evaluation

Your Profile and Agency Preference

So your instructor can arrange agency assignments according to your personal preferences, please fill out this form and hand it in when requested.

Name _____ E-mail address _____

Phone_____ Major _____

My first choice for a client is _____
because (tell why)

My second choice for a client is _____

My first choice for an agency role is _____
because (tell why)

My second choice for an agency role is _____.

My special talents are:

I have read and agree to the agency rules as set forth in the Campaign Planner.

_____
Your signature and date

Developing Agency Relationships: Team-Building Activities

Before meeting for the first time with your agency, try one or more of the exercises below in class to get acquainted with other members and begin building strong working relationships. For more exercises, go to http://www.utdallas.edu/-ajowen/Team.html to download one or more of the entire collection of activities.

1.   ***Backpack Introductions*** allows the group to share information about yourselves by examining the contents of backpacks.

   Directions: Each person takes out three things from his/her backpack that represent something of personal value. Share your possessions and what they mean to you with the group.

2.   ***Reunited*** helps establish what you have in common with the other members of the group.

   Directions: Find ten things you have in common with each other, such as places you've traveled, TV shows you watch, number of siblings, and so forth. Be creative. The first group to come up with ten things wins.

3.   ***Hidden Agenda*** allows everyone to see how agency roles play out.

   Directions: Each person gets a note card with an agency role written on it that he/she must assume and keep secret. The agency is assigned the task of coming up with a short presentation on how to introduce a new service that delivers meals from local restaurants to homes within a ten-mile radius of downtown. Keeping to your role, come up with a name, logo, advertising media, creative concept and an introductory promotional idea. After you complete the task, each person should share his/her role with the group and the frustrations or advantages experienced while sticking to that role.

SECTION III
Keeping Track: Agency Meeting Rosters

Agency Meeting Rosters

These meeting rosters contain information to be covered in the meeting and assignments for the next meeting. For each meeting you attend, fill out the meeting roster as proof of attendance and for information regarding the progress of your Agency.

Before each meeting, be sure to complete the corresponding Step assignment.

Meeting	Topic	Assignment Due	Finish Date
1.	Select Agency Roles		
2.	Situation Analysis	Step 1	_____
3.	Survey Results	Survey	_____
4.	TA & Competition	Steps 2 & 3	_____
5.	Budget & Position	Step s 4 & 5	_____
6.	Comm. Objectives	Step 6	_____
7.	Creative Concepts	Step 7	_____
8.	Media Planning	Step 8	_____
9.	Promotions & Events	Step 9	_____
10.	Evaluation Methods	Step 10	_____

During your first meeting, share information so you will have all agency member's jobs and contact information. You will also select a name and make design suggestions for a logo.

The name of our agency is _____

Member	Agency Role	E-mail and Phone
1.	AE	
&		
2.	Manager	
3.	Researcher	
&		
4.	Media Planner	
5.	Writer	
&		
6.	Artist	
7.	Promotion Director	
&		
8.	PR Director	
9.	Technician	

If your agency is small, allow one person to assume <u>two</u> agency roles. Combine 1 & 2 for the leader, combine 3 & 4 into media & research, combine 5 & 6 for creative, and combine 7 & 8 for promotions. Everyone shares in the technician's job.

Suggestions for a logo design are:

My assignment for the situation analysis research due at the next meeting is:
(circle your assignment)

Industry Overview   Company Profile   Brand Evaluation

Competition Identification

1. Take role. Absent members are:

2. Group members share information on Industry Overview, Company Profile and Brand Evaluation. Using members' input, coordinate your answers to Step 1 in Section IV so everyone has the same information.

3. Decide on where and when to conduct the survey for your client (find the survey in Section V). Research should be completed by the next agency meeting.

   We will conduct the survey at
   _____ location

   by this date _____.

   Each member will hand out and collect _____ copies of the survey.

   After you finish the survey, use the tally sheet on page 75 to total the results from all the surveys you collected. Bring that final tally-survey to the next meeting with your name on it.

4. Decide on a logo for the agency. The technician or the artists will provide each member with a digital logo at the next meeting.

1. Take role. Absent members are:

2. Discuss individual survey results.
   What did you learn?

   What surprised you?

3. Give all survey tallies to the Account Planner who will do a final tally by the next meeting. The AP will also complete the Consumer Attitudes section of Step 1 (p. 39) to share with the group at the next meeting.

4. The AE will assign half the group to complete Step 2 and the other half of the group to complete Step 3.

   I will complete Step _____.

5. Be prepared to share your answers at the next meeting.

1. Take role. Absent members are:

2. Discuss the combined survey results and Section E of Step 1.

3. Conduct a SWOT analysis by reviewing the brand strengths and weaknesses (SW) and evaluating the opportunities and threats (OT) that exist in the marketplace for the brand.

4. This completes the Situation Analysis. The AE will write up your findings for the plans book.

5. Discuss Step 2. Decide on a consumer segment to target. The segment the agency selects can be described as _____ because (tell why):

6. Discuss Step 3. We identify our primary competition to be:

   a.

   b.

   c.

7. Discuss each member's evaluations of your client's brand or product. How were you able to make that evaluation (used it, talked to someone about it, etc.)?

8. The AE will assign half of the agency members to complete Step 4 and the other half to complete Step 5 for the next meeting.

   My assignment is Step _____.

1. Take role. Absent members are:

2. Discuss Step 4. Your agency decides to *allocate the budget* as follows:

   _____ % for media buys   ____ % for event promotion

   _____ % for sales promotions   ____ % Web site
                                        building/maintenance

   _____ % for public relations   ____ % direct mail/database
                                        management

3. Discuss Step 5. The *position strategy* you decide on for your client's brand is _____

   because: (tell why)

4. For the next meeting, everyone will prepare Step 6 to discuss.

1. Take role. Absent members are:

2. Discuss Step 6.
   The main communication objectives of your campaign are:

   a.

   b.

   Because: (tell why)

3. The brand message we decided upon is:

   Because: (tell why)

4. Complete Step 7 for next time. Be prepared to discuss your creative concept suggestions.

MEETING 7: Determine creative strategies

1. Take role. Absent members are:

2. Discuss Step 7. The creative concepts suggested by agency members include:

   a.

   b.

   c.

   d.

3. The Creative Team (Artist and Writer) will work together to execute these concepts for the next meeting. The concepts will be developed in a rough format for agency members to approve before final ads are developed for the Plans Book and the presentation.

4. Complete Step 8 for next time. Be prepared to suggest specific media vehicles to send your advertising message.

1. Take role. Absent members are:

2. Discuss Step 8. The media we will buy for our brand are:

   a.

   b.

   c.

   d.

   Because: (tell why)

   a.

   b.

   c.

   d.

   The Media Planner will prepare a media schedule for the vehicles we suggested above. This schedule will be used for the presentation. S/he will also write the media section of the Plans Book.

3. Complete Step 9 for next time. Bring suggestions for promotions to the next meeting.

1. Take role. Absent members are:

2. The Creative Team will present their executions for the agency to approve or revise. When approved, that team will produce the final ads for the Plans Book and presentation.

   The executions we like best are:

3. Discuss Step 9.

   A. The sales promotions the agency will recommend for a pull strategy are:

      1. Trial_____

      2. Usage_____

   B. Our mailing list will be derived from this source:

      _____

   C. We suggest that our client sponsor the following event (s):

      _____

      because:

Publicity will be achieved by providing a news release to the editors of the_____ section of the newspaper. The subject of the release will be:_____

D. Our suggestions for philanthropy are:

4. The Promotions Director will develop a description of the promotions for the Plans Book and some visuals for the presentation. Use Section V, Execution aids, (page 80-81) to help you plan and event and select a sponsorship opportunity. Include these in your Plans Book.

5. The PR Director will prepare a news release to announce one of the promotions and a charitable association for the Plans Book. Use Section V, Writing a news release, (page 82) to help you prepare the news release for the Plans Book.

6. Prepare Step 10 for the next meeting. Be thinking about who should represent the agency as a presenter of your campaign.

1. Take role. Absent members are:

2. Discuss Step 10. The agency decided to evaluate the campaign using the following methods:

   a.

   b.

   c.

3. We select these two or three agency members to be presenters:

   a.

   b.

   c.

4. Media, Creative, Promotion, and PR people will be ready with their sections of the Plans Book and presentation by the next meeting.

5. Presenters will be prepared to present for the agency at the next meeting. (See Section V, Presentation tips, page 83-84, for hints on presenting your campaign.)

1. Take role. Absent members are:

2. The AE will give completed Sections of the Plans Book to the Productions person for assembling into a bound book. (See Section VI for examples)

3. The presenters will run through their presentation. Agency members will critique the presentation with constructive criticism. Refer to Section IV, Presentation checklist (page 85).

4. Schedule a dress rehearsal for the next meeting if necessary.

   Rehearsal will be conducted at _____

   on this date and time_____

If this is the final meeting, the Plans Book must be completed and ready to turn in to the instructor.

1. Take role. Absent members are:

2. Plans Book must be completed and ready to turn in to the instructor.

   Final responsibility for the Plans Book belongs to

   _____

3. Dress rehearsal is presented and timed.

   Problems identified during the rehearsal are:

CONGRATULATIONS!!! YOU'RE ALMOST FINISHED!!!

Agency Evaluation and Final Report Form

The _____ agency met _____ times to complete

our campaign for (client) _____. Below

is a ranking of members in the order of their effort and dedication to the

project, 1 being the most active. The number of absences of each member is

in parentheses.

1. _____ ( )

2. _____ ( )

3. _____ ( )

4. _____ ( )

5. _____ ( )

6. _____ ( )

7. _____ ( )

Summarize the mood or morale of the agency throughout the campaign
process, noting any problems that surfaced and ways in which they were
addressed (use the reverse side as well).

Evaluated by _____, account manager

SECTION IV
Ten Steps to Building a Great Campaign Plan

Let's get going!!!!

It's the Planning, Stupid!

All campaigns begin the same way: with research and planning. To serve the client well, we must understand our client's industry, the product, and both the competitors and the consumers of this brand. Remember, campaigns are produced to promote a brand in a way that overcomes an identified problem. Without a problem to solve, the client wouldn't need a campaign.

Even successful brands, such as Absolut and Maytag, face new competition and changing technology. To meet such challenges, companies revitalize their ongoing campaigns. Less-successful brands require new campaigns to increase brand awareness or to improve a poor attitude about the brand.

Ten-Step Program

Your workbook contains activities for ten steps. For each step, do these four things:

1. Read the appropriate book chapter from your class textbook.
2. Complete each activity on your own prior to your agency meeting.
3. Meet with your agency and discuss your solutions until you reach consensus among your members.
4. After reaching consensus for the activity, write a short narrative summarizing your findings for use in the Plans Book.

When you have completed all of the activities, your Plans Book will be ready to assemble.

To illustrate how the campaign for TONI&GUY was developed, examples are provided for each activity in shaded areas like this paragraph .

Step 1
Conduct the Situation Analysis

Why conduct a situation analysis for your brand?

Circumstances and events change rapidly in today's marketplace. To be current, agencies must conduct secondary research (data collected by someone else) to determine what economic, social, political, and technological factors will affect strategic elements of the plan. The factors are uncontrollable because we cannot rely on them to remain the same. As our culture grows and changes, so do marketplace factors. These factors help us to determine the environment in which your campaign will be implemented.

In order to complete Step 1, you will need to do the following:

1. Read the chapter in your text that deals with the situation analysis and/or campaign planning.
2. Consult the Internet and other secondary research sources. One of the best ways to proceed is to use http://www.google.com as a search engine to locate information about your client's industry, company, product, and competition. If the client's company is publicly held, you may obtain an annual report from a brokerage company. For a list of useful Web sites for obtaining information relevant to completing Step 1, see Research Aids in Part V.
3. Conduct a short survey to determine brand attitude. Survey protocols can be found in Part V.
4. You may also conduct an information interview with a person at the company for first-hand information about your client's brand (see Page 78 for details on conducting an information interview).

Situation Analysis

Industry Overview

Fill in the blanks with your findings.

The size of your client's industry is computed by sales volume in millions of units or sales in millions of dollars. To understand trends, look at industry sales over a five-year period.

Our client's industry is _____.

Current sales volume is_____

The industry generated sales (in $ millions) during these years:

1999 _____ 2000 _____ 2001_____

2002 _____ 2003_____

Check the descriptor below that best characterizes your client's industry growth:

_____ substantial growth   _____ moderate growth

_____ slow growth   _____ no growth   _____ declining

Economic impacts on the _____ industry are:

[Example: Hair care industry has grown because a bustling economy yields disposable income; prices of hair care products are stable because of substantial competition.]

Social influences on the industry are:

[Example: Increasing attention to appearance has driven the beauty products industry to grow; hair care products are enjoying the same trend.]

Political or governmental regulations on the industry are:

[Example: Testing products on animals is considered bad policy. Government prosecutes counterfeit product makers.]

Technological impacts on the industry are:

[Example: Technology has increased packaging innovations.]

Industry segments. Every industry category can be broken into different segments. List your client's industry segments.

[Example: The personal care industry has hair care products as one of its segments, and hair care can be divided into shampoo, conditioning and styling product segments.]

1.

2.

3.

COMPANY PROFILE

   Locate this information in the company web site or annual report.

The client's company has _____% share of the industry or product category.

Summarize the company's origin, growth and changes (such as acquisition) since its inception.

[Example: See the TiGi company profile in the student Bed Head Campaign Plans Book.]

Brand/Product Evaluation

To do the best job for our client, we must familiarize ourselves with the brand and product in various ways. We gather this information by visiting the location of a service or the place where the product is sold, trying the product first hand, and talking to someone who knows a great deal about it. To understand consumer attitudes about the brand, you will conduct a survey as provided in Part V.

Brands are differentiated from others in the same product category in several ways:

[Example: TiGi's Bed Head and Cat Walk hair care products are distinguished from other brands by their 1) unique packaging, 2) clever names and 3) distinctive Point-Of-Purchase (POP) display case.]

List 3 ways your brand's product is different from other brands' products.

1.

2.

3.

Brands are promoted in the various ways.

[Example: TiGi promotions include 1) placing products in movies, 2) hair styling contests and 3) advertising in fashion magazines.]

List 3 ways your brand is promoted.

1.

2.

3.

List 3 of your brand's *strengths*.

[Example: TiGi's strengths are: 1) strong brand image, 2) good product performance, and 3) global distribution network.]

1.

2.

3.

The brand's **weaknesses** are:

[Example: TiGi weaknesses are 1) vulnerability to competition, 2) mass distribution of Bed Head products, and 3) high prices.]

List 3 of your brand's weaknesses:

1.

2.

3.

Identifying the Competition

Your client's brand falls within the _____ industry segment. Identify three top competitors in this segment.

[Example: TiGi competitors are Aveda, Bumble & Bumble, Paul Mitchell.]

Your client's competitors are:

1.

2.

3.

Consumer Attitudes
(Consumers are surveyed about their awareness and attitudes, and the results are presented in this section)

Top-of-mind awareness is determined by asking category consumers "which brand comes to mind" when they think of the category.

[Example: When you think of hair care products, what brand comes to mind?]

Use the survey protocol found in Section 2 to assess consumer attitudes about your brand, then report the results below.

Rank the top-of-mind awareness levels of these brands according to your survey results. List the highest level first.

[Example: Survey results showed that TiGi brand ranked first, Bumble & Bumble second, and Aveda third among salon owners surveyed.]

1.

2.

3.

o Top-of-Mind awareness of our brand is _____high _____low _____neutral

o Consumers have a generally _____favorable _____unfavorable _____neutral attitude toward the brand.

o Consumers are _____very likely _____likely _____ unlikely _____ very unlikely to use the brand in the near future.

o Consumers of this product category tend to be ____ loyal to the brand _____ switch brands often ____switch brands sometime

When you complete your part of Step 1, share the information with other members of your agency. The combined input will provide vital information for making important decisions in the execution steps.

46

Step 2
Profile the Consumer Segment

Read the chapter in your text that deals with target markets (TM) and consumer segments (CS). A **target market** is the entire group of potential users for your brand, while a **consumer segment** is the special group on which your campaign will focus.

Several factors are used to profile and segment consumers. Consumers can be characterized using:

    1) demographics (age, economic status)
    2) geographics (location)
    3) psychographics (lifestyle)
    4) loyalty (loyal brand user, brand switcher, new user)
    5) usage levels (heavy user, light user)
    6) benefit segments (price, performance, health etc.)

1) Demographics. Give the age range, education level, sex, and income bracket for your target or consumer segment.

[Example: Bed Head is targeted at men and women salon owners 35-50 and stylists 18-32, professionally educated, with an annual income of $40,000.]

Age range _____ Education _____ Sex _____
Income _____

2) Geographics. The location of your consumer segment will define whether or not you buy local or national media. Identify their location.

[Example: Bed Head consumers are global but the test market is local.]

3) Psychographics. SRI Inc. has developed the Values And LifeStyles (VALS) system to classify American consumers. To learn about the system and to discover your own segment classification, log on to the site http://www.sri.com and click on "take the survey." After you answer the questions, enter your e-mail address and press the enter/return button. You will receive your profile immediately. Then visit the "description" portion of the site, or read the chapter in your text on VALS, to understand how consumer lifestyles are determined.

The VALS profile(s) that pertain to our consumer segment is (are):

Next, characterize the lifestyle of the consumer segment according to their habits. List the lifestyle characterization of your brand's consumer segment:

[Example: Stylists are achievers who want a product their clients can use to reflect status and self-esteem.]

4) **Loyalty.** People who use or buy a particular brand category are labeled four ways.

- Brand loyals (BL) are people who like and buy the brand; they are a preferred segment since we don't have to sell them on purchasing our products.

- Other brand loyals (OBL), on the other hand, are the hardest to sell and the least likely to change to our brand; we usually don't target this group.

- Brand switchers come in two varieties, *favorable* (FBS) and *unfavorable* (UBS). Both are influenced by cost and price promotions in making their brand decisions . We target these groups with promotions in the hope they will become BLs.

- Consumers who do not use or buy products in our category are called non-category users. In most cases, we avoid this group unless they are not users because of age. Then they become new category users (NCU); we target them in the hopes they will try our brand when they mature into the brand category.

The best loyalty segment for this campaign is _____.

5) **Usage.** Define your primary target market as heavy, regular, light, or occasional users according how often they buy the brand.

[Example: Salon stylists are heavy users of Bed Head styling products.]

Our consumers are _____ users of _____.

48

6) Benefit Segments. Consumers can also be characterized by the benefits they prefer from each brand in the category. In the toothpaste category, smokers may prefer whiteners (Remington's), mothers may prefer decay-fighting paste (Crest), teens often want breath fresheners (AquaFresh), health-conscious brushers want natural ingredients (Tom's of Maine), many buy on price (store brand), and others want the convenience of an upright dispenser (MentaDent).

[Bed Head Example:]	
Brand category benefit	**Brand that has it**
packaging	Bed Head
quality	Bumble & Bumble
natural ingredients	Aveda
not tested on animals	Body Shop
price	Paul Mitchell
aroma	Aveda, Bed Head

List all the benefits associated with your brand category and the brand that has each benefit, and identify which benefit your consumer segment prefers.

Brand category benefit	**Brand that has it**

1.

2.

3.

4.

Our Consumer Segment prefers the _____ benefit.

Media contacts, the places where brand messages might intersect with your campaign's consumer segment, are important for identifying potential media placement. Think about all the places your consumer segment will intersect with brand messages.

> *[Example: Teens see Bed Head magazine ads, Web site, and sponsorship logos; adults see displays, ads, posters, salon displays, and Web sites.]*

(Our brand's messages should include these places.)

1.

2.

3.

A good way of summarizing all the traits of your consumers is to write out a short statement profiling your campaign's consumer segment. Use the TiGi plans book example as your guide.

Go on to step 3.

Step 3
Analyze the Competition

Read the chapter in your text that deals with product positioning.

For each competitor you identified in Step 1, list their major promotion vehicle(s).

[Bed Head Example:]	
Competitor	**Promotion Vehicles**
Bumble and Bumble	Little League sponsorship
Aveda	Campaign against animal testing
Paul Mitchell	**Retail sales incentives**

Competitor	Promotion Vehicles

1.

2.

3.

For each competitor, locate the slogan or advertising campaign theme.

[Bed Head Example:]	
Competitor	**Slogan/Campaign Theme**
Bumble	Understated elegance
Aveda	Serving the environment
Paul Mitchell	Follow the leader

Competitor	Slogan/Campaign Theme

1.

2.

3.

Each competitor has a strength that is often used to differentiate itself from the rest of the brands in the same category.

[Bed Head Example:]	
Competitor	**_Brand Position_**
Aveda	All natural ingredients
Bumble & Bumble	First in fashion
Paul Mitchell	Industry pioneer

Tell how each of your client's competitors positions itself.

Competitor	_Brand Position_

1.

2.

3.

Competitors' products have both strengths and weaknesses.

[Bed Head Example:]		
Competitor	**_Strength_**	**_Weakness_**
Aveda	Market niche	Not in most salons
Bumble & Bumble	Trendy	Poor packaging
Paul Mitchell	Brand recognition	High prices

For each of your client's competitors, list its most important strength and weakness.

Competitor	_Strength_	_Weakness_

1.

2.

3.

During the next meeting, you and your agency should make personal comparisons among the competitors and share your experiences, both positive and negative, when you discuss the competition and its role for planning and executing your campaign.

Step 4
Allocate the Budget

Budgets are determined in a variety of ways, most of which are discussed in your textbook. A common method is called "percentage of future sales". For the sake of this campaign, use 10% of the most recent sales revenues to allocate your budget spending. For instance, Starbucks' worldwide sales revenues for 2004 were projected to be $4.2 billion. Ten percent of that amount, $42 million, is the budget allocated to prepare an *international* campaign. If this is a *regional* campaign or a *test market*, use 2% of the national sales revenues for your campaign. If you have a *local* client, use 6% of their anticipated sales for the coming year as your budget.

Your campaign budget is $_____.

Because we are working with a specific dollar amount, you must prioritize which aspects of the campaign will receive the biggest share of the budget.

[Example: (see Bed Head Plans Book)]
With a budget of $200,000 to promote Bed Head Boutiques to salon owners, stylists and consumers, we allocate the following expenditures:
- 50% or $100,000 for promotion and merchandising.
- 40% or $40, 000 to media buying.
- 10% or $10,000 for public relations.

Using a pie chart, allocate your approximate budget in percentages. You may decide to reconfigure these amounts after completing the Execution Steps. For now, these amounts will serve as guidelines and approximate proportions.

Step 5
Establish a Brand Positioning Strategy

A brand's **position** is its place in the mind of the consumer with regard to all the other brands in this category. Several strategic positioning options are available to you. Here are some examples of how positioning statements are presented by brand strategy.

Write a position statement for each example below.

1. Position the brand against its major competitor.
   [Example: Stylists prefer Bed Head above all other products.]

2. Position the brand away from the others in the category.
   [Example: Bed Head product boutiques give salons a distinctive status.]

3. Position the brand as the category leader.
   [Example: Bed Head is number one in styling products.]

4. Position the brand to a specific Consumer Segment.
   [Example: A Bed Head Boutique gives status to salon owners.]

5. Position the brand as unique.
   [Example: No other hair care products combine humor with packaging and presentation.]

My agency's brand will use the position strategy illustrated in option # _____ above because (justify your choice):

Write out a positioning statement for the positioning strategy you have chosen.

[Example: Globally and locally, Bed Head will remain the leading hair styling product among consumers and hair stylists alike. Bed Head Boutiques will identify premium salons.]

Step 6
Determine the Communication Objectives and Advertising Message

Communication Objectives

Campaigns meet or establish various kinds of objectives. *Marketing objectives* are set based on sales, profits, or share of market; they have either a dollar value or percentage rate. *Campaign objectives* are based on brand message delivery, not dollars. A campaign is determined successful if the communication objectives are met. *Communication objectives* are measurable and can be evaluated by measuring pre- and post-campaign levels. A successful campaign achieves its communication objectives. They are:

1. **Category Need.** The "Got Milk" campaign message was delivered to build category need by establishing the value of drinking milk. The emphasis of the advertising message is on the category, not the brand.

2. **Brand Awareness.** Most campaigns include this objective, and some campaigns focus exclusively on creating or maintaining brand awareness. Awareness is measured by brand recognition and brand recall. *Recognition objectives* are concerned with introducing the brand mark or logo to the target audience so that the brand is recognized at the time of purchase. When we see a particular brand on a store shelf, we recognize it. *Recall objectives* work to put the brand in the minds of consumers prior to purchase. When we make out a shopping list, we identify the brand before going to market.

3. **Brand Attitude.** Consumer attitudes about the brand can be created (for new brands), changed (from bad to good) or maintained. A campaign message aimed at other brand users must change attitudes toward our brand. Campaign messages aimed at loyal users will reinforce consumers' positive brand feelings.

4. **Brand Purchase Intention.** The only way behaviors can be changed is to stimulate a consumer's intention to buy the brand. This objective is designed to stimulate purchase through an incentive such as a coupon or a limited-time offer. To stimulate sales, advertising messages will announce 10% off on all products for the month of February.

5. **Brand Purchase Facilitation**. This objective is used when additional information is necessary to complete the purchase process. An advertising message may include a Web site address for consumers to find a retail location to buy the brand.

Advertising Message

An advertising message is carried throughout the campaign in every medium and delivery system. To create your client's advertising message, use the format illustrated below.

> **[Example]**
> **Advertising will <u>create recall awareness</u> among <u>new users</u> that**
>   communication objective   usage segment
>
> **<u>Bed Head</u> is <u>preferred by more hair stylists than any other brand</u>.**
>   our brand   position statement

Remember, your advertising message is specific to the consumer segment. If you have two segments to target, you will need two distinct and separate advertising messages.

To create an advertising message for your client's brand, select a communication objective, a consumer segment, and a position statement and fill in the blanks below.

Advertising will _____among _____
                    communication objective   usage segment

that _____is _____.
        our brand   position statement

Refer to this message when developing the next three execution steps. Media objectives, creative strategy, and promotional objectives should take their direction from this message statement.

Step 7
Develop the Creative Strategy

After reading about creative strategies in your textbook, consider some of the options available for structuring print and broadcast advertising. Log on to http://www.adcritic.com for an archive of great TV commercials that will stimulate your creative juices.

Identify Attributes, Benefits and Values

Advertisers use the "Means End Chain" to determine how consumer needs and wants can be used for creative executions. Identifying your product's best attributes is the first step in determining a creative strategy. An *attribute* is a tangible or innate feature that makes the product different from all the rest. The *benefit* is what the consumer gets from using that feature. Ultimately, consumers use the product because of a particular subconscious *value*. Creative messages should translate what your product has into what the user gets. Complete the chart below for your product or service.

	[Bed Head Example:]	
ATTRIBUTE	**BENEFIT**	**VALUE**
What the product has	**What the user gets**	
Creative packaging	Stylish bottles	Design
Variety of ingredients	Special products	Quality
Economical price	Savings	Economy
Technological advances	Great hair styles	Self-esteem

Your product's attributes	Benefits	Values
1.		
2.		
3.		

Choose a Hero

Choosing a hero for your creative executions involves deciding between the product and the user as the star of the advertisement or commercial.

- When your product or service solves problems that benefit a user (like a credit card), or has a unique attribute (like 4-wheel drive), the **product is the hero**.
- When your product is like most of the others in the same category (such as batteries or beer), the **user is the hero.**
- If your client is a corporation where brand image is the strategy (like Microsoft), the **brand is the hero**.

When a product, brand or service is the hero, the brand/product is the dominant visual:

[Example: When Bed Head <u>products</u> are heroes (the ingredients and packaging signal quality), we feature the package.
When TiGi <u>brand</u> is the hero (it offers free training for salon stylists), we feature the brand mark.
When TONY&GUY <u>salon services</u> are heroes (they provide the latest hairstyles and styling products), we feature a salon logo.]

Our client is a hero because:

When the product or service user is the hero, the target audience is the dominant visual:

[Example: When we want to convey that salon stylists get more client satisfaction when they use Bed Head products, we feature satisfied stylists. The stylist is a hero because s/he uses the product. The benefit received is a happy customer and attractiveness is the value. The beautiful client and happy stylist are featured visuals in the advertisement or commercial.]

Our users are heroes because:

Develop the Creative Concept

Remember, in a campaign, you're not designing one advertisement, you are creating a concept that will deliver the promotional message in every medium and execution throughout the entire campaign. Think of the concept as the campaign's *unifying element.*

A concept can be a sign, such as the "milk mustache", an icon such as the Pillsbury Dough Boy, a musical element or sound like Pepsi's "whooosh," a theme like Master Card's "priceless" campaign, or a slogan like L'Oreal's "Because I'm worth it."

What is your campaign's unifying element? Why?

The most effective way to develop a creative strategy is with a *Creative Brief*. Working as a team, the account executive and account planner develop an outline for the creative team. The Creative Brief involves answering the following questions:

- What is the opportunity or problem the advertising must address?
- What do we want to do as a result of the advertising?
- Who are we talking to?
- What is the key response we want?
- What information/attributes might help produce this response?
- What aspect of the brand's personality should advertising express?
- Are there media or budget considerations?
- What other information might affect the creative direction?

[Example: Turn to the TONY&GUY creative brief in Section VI, p. 23].

When your agency meets, work with your AE and planner to develop a Creative Brief for your brand.

60

Step 8
Set Media Objectives and Strategies

Reach and Frequency Objectives

Effective campaigns must reach a consumer segment with enough promotional message repetitions to achieve the communications objective(s). Delivering a broad reach and frequent impressions is very expensive. Budget allocations are established to maintain a balance between reach and frequency.

A *reach priority* is used when:
- your objective is brand recognition.
- your brand is national.
- your consumers are diverse.
- your product has a short life-cycle.

The best media vehicles for a reach strategy are network television, magazines, outdoor boards, and a Web site.

A *frequency priority* is used when:
- your objective is brand recall.
- your product or service is directed to a special consumer segment.

Frequency is best achieved by using cable television, radio, newspapers, and a Web site.

For our client, _____ will be our priority.

Media Selection Strategy

In order to be received, the promotional message must be delivered to the target audience through the medium that your consumer segment uses most often. To determine which media are appropriate for your segment, consult syndicated sources like Simmons, or conduct a focus group with members of that segment to see what they read, watch and listen to, and how often.

[Example: TONI&GUY targets salon owners through trade publications.]

For your consumer segment, determine which media are used and how often they're needed by checking the appropriate column.

Medium	Usage		
	Seldom	*Usually*	*Always*
Newspaper			
Magazines			
Network TV			
Cable TV			
Outdoor			
Radio			
Internet			
Movies (for product placements)			

After you make a media selection, consider specific *vehicles* for each medium.

- For network television or radio, vehicles are the *programs* your users watch.
- For newspapers and magazines, vehicles are the *periodicals* your users read.

For each medium you checked in the *usually or always* columns above, suggest two or three specific vehicles your consumer segment uses.

Medium	**Vehicles**

1.

2.

3.

Example: See the Media Plan for TONI&GUY in the student Plans Book.)

Step 9
Create Rewarding Promotions

In addition to buying advertising for media, you can deliver messages to consumers in a variety of unique ways. Select the strategies from those discussed that will best deliver the campaign's promotional message.

Sales Promotions

Sales promotions are designed for both retailers and consumers. We have two promotional strategies from which to choose, push and pull. We *push* our promotions onto retailers who in turn push the brand to consumers. And we *pull* consumers to our brand by offering price promotions directly to them.

Sales promotion tactics used with a *push strategy* encourage retailers to push your products to the client. Those tactics include:
- Trade promotions
- Product demonstrations
- Collateral materials
- Instruction and education
- Sales incentives
- Cooperative advertising
- Contests

Suggest a push tactic for your client _____.

Sales promotion tactics used with a *pull strategy* are used to stimulate trial and usage among consumers. Trial and usage are promotional objectives.

Tactics used to stimulate *trial* among non-users include:
- Coupons.
- Sampling.
- Sweepstakes.
- Guarantees.
- Rebates.

We recommend the following tactics to stimulate trial for our client's brand _____.

Tactics used to increase *usage* among current brand users include:
- Coupons.
- Contests.
- Warranties.
- Premiums.

We recommend the following tactics to increase usage among consumers of our brand: _____

Data Based Marketing

Taking your product or brand message to the consumer without using a mass medium requires data based marketing. Companies can develop their own consumer lists or buy them from a list distributor, or purchase them from magazine or catalog publishers.

Direct mail is one method of marketing directly to the consumer using the post office. Zip codes mailings target local consumers for retailers or service organizations.
Internet messages can be directed toward consumer e-mail addresses. These can be purchased the same way as home addresses—through a variety of list providers.

Suggest the best way to obtain a mail or Internet database for your consumer segment.

Sponsorships

By sponsoring sporting and cultural events, brand messages can be delivered to consumers indirectly by connecting the brand with an activity they enjoy. Equipment companies (Nike) sponsor sporting events, beverage companies (Coke) sponsor musical events, and oil companies (Unocal) sponsor art exhibitions. The key to success is pairing the right event with your brand. Use the sponsorship aid found in Part IV to help you evaluate the available alternatives.

Suggest a sponsor for your client and provide a rationale for your choice.

Public Relations

Public relations involves dealing with the various "publics" of a corporation, such as stockholders, employees, government, media and consumers. One aspect of public relations is publicity. Campaigns use publicity to present the brand or product to the public as news or a feature story. The sports section often contains a review of a new car model, or the travel writer recommends a specific hotel. These features are planted with editors by publicists.

Publicity is achieved by sending or delivering a news release to newspaper or television editors. The message must be newsworthy and must appeal to the editor's readers.

A sample news release is provided on Page 82. What feature or news angle can you suggest for a news release about your brand or client?

Philanthropy

Companies that give back to the community improve their image while continuing to create awareness and build good will among its various publics. "Cause marketing" is the term used for endorsing a worthwhile issue. Chevron's "People Do" campaign promotes wildlife conservation. AIDS walks and cancer marathons have corporate sponsors to help them raise funds in exchange for logo visibility. Financial companies often sponsor a public broadcast network's programming.

Suggest a cause, charity, or activity that will benefit your brand through such an association.

Step 10
Set Evaluation Criteria

Every campaign plan must include a method for determining whether or not its objectives have been met. Each objective is evaluated by conducting tests or measuring performance.

Communication objectives can be measured in these ways:

- **Category need**. Measure the number of category users before and after the campaign.
    Method: Pre-post surveys.
- **Awareness—recognition.** Measure the number of people who recognize the brand before and after the campaign.
    Method: Pre-post surveys.
- **Awareness—recall.** Measure the number of people who name the brand without prompting before and after the campaign.
    Method: Top-of-mind awareness pre-post questions.
- **Attitude.** Measure the attitude of consumers prior to and after the campaign.
    Method: Pre-post scaling questions about consumer perceptions of the brand.
- **Brand purchase intention**. Measure the likelihood of purchasing the brand before and after the campaign promotions.
    Method: Ask consumer segment how likely they are to purchase the product within the next month.

Media objectives can be measured in the following ways:

1. Expected Gross Rating Points (GRPs) compared with actual GRPs.
    Method: Neilson syndicated research.
2. Expected circulation compared with actual circulation.
    Method: Audit Bureau of Circulation report.
3. Expected impressions compared with actual impressions.
    Method: Insertion reports, tear sheets.

Sales promotions can be measured by:

1. The number of coupons redeemed.
2. The number of premiums ordered.
3. The number of special offers accepted within the time period.

SECTION V
Campaign Aids and Activities

Research Aids

Web Sites

Log on to the following Web sites to obtain relevant information about your client's industry, company, market, and competitors.

http://www.about.com—This site includes evaluations of more than 650 subject areas. For each area, a personal contact is provided.

http://www.bd.dowjones.com—Dow Jones has created a great business subject directory.

http://www.bizreport.com—Daily Internet business reports, marketing, research, and insight are reported here along with international sections.

http://www.britannica.com—This site has an extensive subject directory based on Britannica's encyclopedia with page links to more than 130,000 sites.

http://www.business.com—Provides business information by industry. Offers key players, events, associations, in-depth profiles, stock quotes and statistics, competitive analysis and real-time news of top stories, company, and global news.

http://www.companysleuth.com—Company Sleuth offers free daily reports about public US companies, including stock quotes and job listings.

http://www.hoovers.com—Includes company descriptions, information about key competitors, rankings and current news related to the company.

http://www.brandweek.com—Provides all the latest news on branding.

http://www.brandchannel.com—A good source for branding profiles.

http://www.adage.com—A monthly advertising trade publication with campaign reviews on a global basis.

http://www.adweek.com—A weekly advertising trade publication with industry insights on a regional basis.

These sites will connect you with **advertising associations** that provide services and resources you may need for your campaign.

http://www.aaaa.org—American Association of Advertising Agencies
http://www.aaf.org—American Advertising Federation
http://www.aef.com—American Education Foundation
http://www.iaa.com—International Advertising Association

Survey Instruments

Surveys serve the purpose of gathering primary data for use in the Plans Book. The information collected helps the agency determine the top-of-mind brand awareness of college students, descriptors that indicate their attitudes about the brand, and an indication of whether or not they intend to try the brand.

If each team member copies 20 surveys to pass out, the agency will have at least 100 surveys to use for this research exercise.

Use a clean copy of the survey to total responses of the 20 surveys you collect. A tally sheet is located at the end of this section. Fill it out prior to your next agency meeting. The Account Planner will collect the tally sheets for a final survey total.

Prior to handing out surveys, ask a qualifying question to be certain that each respondent is a brand category user. For instance, "Do you drink Energy Drinks?" or "Do you play golf?" or "Do you watch public broadcasting?" or "Do you download music from the Internet?" If you receive a *no* answer to the qualifying question, do not distribute the survey. Instead, find another person who answers *yes* to the qualifying question to complete the survey.

Survey on Energy Drinks

My class is researching student attitudes and preferences regarding energy drinks. Please take a few minutes to fill out this survey.

1. When you think of energy drinks, what brand comes to mind?

   _____

2. Tell how important each item is to you when buying energy drinks by **writing in the correct number.**

Very important	Somewhat Important	Not important
5	3	1

   _____ taste   _____ ingredients (all natural, vitamins)

   _____ price   _____ recommendation from an athlete

   _____ size   _____ well-known brand

3. **Circle the adjectives** that best describe your attitudes about Monster Energy Drink.

   unknown   trendy   wonderful   expensive   tasty

   athletes' drink harmful   useless   overrated

4. Put an X beside the incentive that might tempt you to consider trying Monster Energy Drink.

   _____ $1.00 off coupon   _____ free logo T-shirt

   _____ trial membership   _____ promotional music
              in a sports club   CD or cassette

5. How likely are you to buy a bottle of Monster Energy Drink in the next few weeks? (circle one)

   very likely   likely   unlikely   very unlikely

6. Circle the words that best describe you:

   Male   sophomore   senior
   Female   freshman   junior   non-student

Survey on Golf Clubs

My class is researching student attitudes and preferences regarding golf clubs. Please take a few minutes to fill out this survey.

1. When you think of golf clubs or balls, what brand comes to mind?

    _____

2. Tell how important each item would be to you when buying clubs by **writing in the correct number.**

Very important 5	Somewhat Important 3	Not important 1
_____ brand	_____ strength	_____ celebrity endorsement
_____ cost	_____ reputation	_____ feel

3. **Circle the adjectives** that best describe your attitude about golf.

    exciting   old-person's game   fun to watch   fun to play

    hard to learn   expensive   challenging   who cares?

4. If you take up golf, how likely are you to consider Callaway golf clubs? (circle one)

    very likely   likely   unlikely   very unlikely

5. Circle the words that best describe you:

    male   sophomore   senior

    female   freshman   junior   nonstudent

My class is researching student attitudes and preferences regarding Internet music download providers. Please take a few minutes to fill out this survey.

1. When you think of music provider companies, which brand comes to mind?

   _____

2. Tell how important each item is to you when paying to download music online by **writing in the correct number**.

Very important	Somewhat Important	Not important
5	3	1

   _____ ease of access   _____ price of song

   _____ membership options   _____ other products

   _____ reputation   _____ selection

3. **Circle the adjectives** that best describe your attitude about purchasing music on line.

   troublesome   easy to do   economical   expensive

   unreliable   complicated   technology restrictive   wonderful

4. How likely are you to download music from Napster in the next month? (circle one)

   very likely   likely   unlikely   very unlikely

5. Circle the words that best describe you:

   male   sophomore   senior

   female   freshman   junior   nonstudent

Survey on Public Broadcasting

My class is researching student attitudes and preferences regarding public broadcasting. Please take a few minutes to fill out this survey.

1. When you think of public broadcasting, what brand comes to mind?

   _____

2. Tell how important each item is to you when considering whether or not to watch public television programming by **writing in the correct number**.

Very important	Somewhat Important	Not important
5	3	1

   _____ education   _____ adventure _____ sit-coms

   _____ reality shows   _____ news   _____ sport

3. **Circle the adjectives** that best describe your attitude about watching public television.

   for kids boring   educational   informative   unimportant

   wonderful   colorless   invisible   entertaining   bothersome

4. How likely are you to listen to a PBS station in the next month? (circle one)

   very likely   likely   unlikely   very unlikely

5. Circle the words that best describe you:

   male   sophomore   senior

   female   freshman   junior   nonstudent

My class is researching student attitudes and preferences regarding online bookstores. Please take a few minutes to fill out this survey.

1. When you think of your brand/company, what brand comes to mind?

_____

2. Tell how important each item is to you when choosing your brand or client by writing in the correct number.

Very important	Somewhat Important	Not important
5	3	1

In this section, list 6 or so features and/or benefits of your product or service.

3. Circle the adjectives that best describe your attitude about your brand or product.

In this section, list 8 or 10 adjectives that apply to the product or brand category, both positive and negative.

4. How likely are you to buy the brand or use the service in the next month? (circle one)

very likely   likely   unlikely   very unlikely

5. Circle the words that best describe you:

male   sophomore   senior

female   freshman   junior   nonstudent

Fill out this sheet to determine survey results. The Account Planner will prepare the narrative for the Plans Book using graphs to visually explain the team's collective results.

1. List the top 5 brands mentioned and rank them in order of how many times they were mentioned in all of the surveys.

   a. _____   b. _____   c._____

   d. _____   e. _____

2. For each item in this question, total all the numbers. List them here from highest number to lowest number.

   a.   e.   i.

   b.   f.   j.

   c.   g.   k.

   d.   h.   l.

3. For each adjective, count the number of time it is checked. List the adjectives in order from highest to lowest number.

   a.   e.   i.

   b.   f.   j.

   c.   g.   k.

   d.   h.   l.

4. For each answer, total the likelihood of using the client's brand .

   Very likely _____Likely _____ Unlikely _____ Very unlikely_____

5. Count and total the items circled and list them with those totals.
   _____male   _____female

   _____freshman _____sophomore _____jr. _____sr. _____non-student

Helpful Hints

Tips for Planning an Event

Events create brand awareness and a favorable brand attitude. Event planning is a time-consuming activity that requires careful coordination and responsible people. Events are held for specific reasons, most of them tied to forming a positive attitude about the sponsor. Here are some suggestions for planning a successful event:

- Select an event that appeals directly to your target audience or the people you want to become aware of your brand. Energy drink companies might schedule a sport competition, a golf equipment company can organize a game between TV stations, PBS may sponsor an art auction, and an online music distributor is likely to prefer promoting concerts.

- Pick a time and location that conform to the participants' schedules and preferences.

- Estimate the number of people you'd like to attend.

- Estimate the cost of your event, including the following expenses:
  $ _____Venue rental fees
  $_____Tables/chairs/furniture rental fees
  $_____Food/beverage and/or catering costs (per person)
  $_____Entertainment charges
  $_____Parking fees
  $_____Advertising rates
  $_____Management and coordination costs
  $_____Servers and cleaners hourly rate
  $_____Media coverage (PR firm or coordinator)
  $_____Total (approximate)

- These expenses make up your total budget. This budget should be considered as part of your promotion expenses (specifically PR).

Remember, only schedule and plan an event that will achieve a communication objective for the brand. Random events with no other purpose than to have fun are discouraged.

Tips for Selecting Sponsors and Partners

Another way to build awareness and create a favorable brand attitude is to sponsor a group or team event. Beer companies sponsor sporting events and large corporations sponsor cultural and performing arts events.

Always select an activity or sport that
- your target audience prefers.
- lends itself well to your client's business.
- has high visibility.
- is consistent with your client's past sponsorships.

Partnerships work by packaging several brands together for a joint promotion. American Express, American Airlines, Hertz Rental Car, and Marriott Hotels have packaged vacations that feature all four travel-related brands.

Always select a partner that
1. enhances the image of your client's brand.
2. consumers consider equivalent in quality to your client's brand.
3. offers complimentary services or products to your client's brand.
4. has the potential to foster a lasting and mutually beneficial relationship.

Tips for Writing a News Release

News releases require a special format and are usually printed on your agency's or client's letterhead with the word NEWS in large letters near the top of the page. When preparing a news release, follow these directions:

- Start the news 1/3 of the way down the page.
- Type headline in all capital letters and underlined.
- Begin the narrative with the city where the release was written and the date, then a colon.
- Double space the body of the release, indent paragraphs, and do not split paragraphs from one page to the next.
- At the end of the page, write –more- to indicate that another page follows.
- Use the symbols ### at the end of the release.

NEWS

Agency or Client Name
Address
Contact: (sender's name)
Phone: FOR IMMEDIATE RELEASE

HEADLINE GOES HERE IN ALL CAPS, UNDERLINED AND CENTERED

HOLLYWOOD, April 1: Double space the body of your release for readability and to permit editing by the receiver.

Use normal indents and consistent spacing between paragraphs. Present all information in descending order of importance, ending with the least important items. Remember, this is news about the brand, not an advertisement. Use the third person, and be objective and factual.

###

How to Ask for the Order:
The Art of Presenting

Why we present and who we present to

Presentations are made for four reasons: to **update** an audience on a project or event, to **explain** how to carry out a procedure, to **motivate** listeners to take action, and—our purpose—to **persuade** listeners to accept your proposal as the best solution to their campaign needs.

Our audiences are the client and your professor. The presentation must demonstrate your knowledge of advertising for your professor, and must convince the client that your ideas are based on strategies that meet brand objectives. Also you must convince both audiences that your media, creative, and promotional ideas are unique and focused on achieving objectives in a measurable and timely fashion.

Use your memory or PowerPoint

You must decide on what method of delivery the agency will use: memorization, speaking from notes, or speaking with the use of a PowerPoint Presentation.

The most effective method for business presentations is speaking from an outline in the form of computer-generated slides. The spontaneous, conversational quality of speaking without notes builds audience rapport and results in a superior presentation.

Never read your slides; use broad topics rather than sentences or paragraphs. If your audience is reading your slides, they're not listening to you.

Review the PowerPoint presentation example in Part VI for Bed Head products asan example of how to abbreviate the amount of information included in each slide.

Use an easy-to-follow format

Every presentation has three parts: opening, body, and closing. The *opening* must capture the interest of your client immediately. For a proposal, you need not only the audience's attention but also their cooperation to implement your proposal.

Some of the best ways to *open* are:

Ask a question: *If we were able to increase your brand's awareness by 60% over the next six months for a very small budget, how happy would you be?*

Give a startling fact: *During the next 24 hours, 136 million people will be choosing a new brand of shampoo.*

Use a dramatic prop or visual aid: (holding up two styling products) *Both of these products style hair, but only one contains no harmful chemicals.*

Quote a well-known person: *Woody Allen says that 98% of the job is just showing up.*

Once you have their attention, let the audience know the scope of your remarks: "*Our presentation covers four aspects of the campaign, situation analysis, creative, media, and promotion.*"

The content of your proposal comes in the *body* where you develop the points introduced in the opening. Use specific evidence, examples, implications, consequences, and other information. Present these in a logical sequence that leads up to the most important part, the campaign's *big idea*.

- Establish your credibility by convincing the client that you've done a thorough job of collecting and analyzing the data and that your points are reasonable. Support your arguments with credible evidence—survey results, statistics, sample quotes, and industry data. Don't inundate the listener with too many facts—they are provided in the Plans Book. Just offer an overview of the important highlights.

- Deal with negative information by acknowledging the problems up front. Confine your discussion to the communication aspects, not the product features.

- Talk to the audience, not to the slide or visual. Stand to the right of the screen and point with your right hand or use a laser pointer. Be careful not to turn your back on the audience.

The *ending* is your last opportunity to ask for the business. You should summarize your points and leave the audience with a clear and simple message. Your audience will remember best what you say last, so finish on a very upbeat note. Don't forget to ask for the business. Tell the client that you are looking forward to working with him/her and that you want your ideas implemented.

Overall

1. Use a presenter for each section—the AE should introduce the team and deliver the start. The account planner will profile the consumer and discuss the research conducted by the agency. The media, creative and promotion spokespeople should each provide a visual to explain their part of the proposal.

2. Rehearse your presentation several times, the last time in front of other students. Check their reactions and get feedback on how you can improve your delivery.

3. Check your equipment prior to your presentation. Technology should not be your enemy!

To avoid surprises, always rehearse

> Practice with your PowerPoint and check the technology.
> Deliver a professional presentation

Must-do rules for success
- Dress appropriately. A themed fashion or professional attire is best.
- Use simple language and short sentences.
- Stand tall and speak clearly.
- Maintain eye contact with the audience.
- Plan answers to possible questions ahead of time.

Xtracredit Assignment

Information Interview

Information interviews are important as a fact-gathering activity to learn more about a client or a specific agency role. When you interview someone in your client's industry or in the advertising/ promotion business, you obtain knowledge that might not be available from reports or university sources.

Here are the steps needed to plan and execute an information interview for your client or to learn about an agency position.

Call for an appointment.

- When calling a client, you may want to speak to a secretary or a salesperson first to see who might provide the best source of information.
- Locate an agency in the phone book or from the Directory of Advertising Agencies and ask the receptionist to connect you with a specific department or position representative (creative department; account coordinator) who will talk to you, a student.
- When you are connected, introduce yourself as a student and explain the purpose of your request.
- Ask for a 15–30 minute interview, no more.

Be prepared with background information.

- When talking to a company or agency, consult the pertinent Web site, magazine article or annual report so you know about that company or agency prior to the interview.

The more up-front knowledge you have, the better you can direct your questions. And the better you look to the client.

Develop your interview questions

Use your background knowledge to begin the interview:

> <u>To a client:</u>
> "I understand that your company's brand is a leader in its category. Can you tell me why?"
>
> <u>To an agency person:</u>
> "Your agency's ads won a Clio Award. What role did you as creative director play in getting that award?"

Ask open-ended questions that can't be answered with one word.

> <u>To a client:</u>
> "Tell me how your company got started."
>
> <u>To an agency person:</u>
> "Explain how you got from college to your current job position."

Rehearse your questions and weed out the ones that can be answered by checking another source.

DON'T ASK
- <u>A client</u> "What year did your company go public?"

- <u>An agency person</u>: "How many clients does your agency have?"

Such questions are published and readily available elsewhere.

Meet with your contact
- Dress professionally. You are only taken as seriously as you take your own appearance.
- Use a tape recorder so you can listen and replay the answers. Avoid taking notes that divert your attention from the person.
- Stay within your appointment time; remember, these people are busy and have given freely of their time.

Write up an interview summary
- Summarize the important points made in the interview for use in your campaign Plans Book or for future reference.
- Include the date, time and place of the interview, and the interviewees name, title or position, and company or agency.

Client/Agency Information Interview
Visitation Report

Date_____Interviewer_____

Name of person interviewed_____

Title and company of person interviewed_____

Describe your impression of the company/agency you visited based on its physical appearance and the appearances of the people employed there.

Summarize what you learned about the company, agency, or position during the interview.

Hand this form into your instructor.

Books to Read
Advertising and the Business of Branding

Aitchison, Jim. *How Asia Advertises*. Boston: John Wiley, 2002.

Basksin, Merry, Mark Earls, and Dominic Mills, eds. *Brand New Brand Thinking*. Kogan Page, 2003.

Bedbury, Scott. *A New Brand World*. Viking, 2002.

Berger, Arthur Asa. *Ads, Fads and Consumer Culture,* 2nd ed. Rowman & Littlefield, . 2004.

Blackwell, Roger and Tina Staphan. *Brands that Rock*. Boston: John Wiley, 2004.

Gad, Thomas. *4-D Branding.* Prentice-Hall, 2001.

Gottdiener, Mark. *The Theming of America: Dreams, Visions and Commercial Spaces*. Westview Press, 1997.

Ind, Nicholas. *Great Advertising Campaigns: Goals and Accomplishments*. New York: McGraw-Hill, 2000.

Lois, George. *What's the Big Idea? How to Win with Outrageous Ideas that Sell*. Doubleday Currency, 1991.

Ogilvy, David. *Ogilvy on Advertising.* Vintage Press, 1985.

Parente, Donald. *Ad Campaign Strategy: A Guide to Marketing Communication Plans,* 3rd ed. International Tompson, 2003.

Pricken, Mario. *Creative Advertising: Ideas and Techniques from the World's Best Campaigns*. Thomas & Hudson, 2004.

Pringle, Hamish and Marjorie Thompson. *Brand Spirit*. Boston: John Wiley, 2001.

Steel, Jon. *Truth, Lies & Advertising: The Art of Account Planning.* Boston: John Wiley, 1998.

Southerland, Max and Alice Sylvester. *Advertising and the Mind of the Consumer,* 2nd ed. Independent Publishing Group, 2000.

Underhill, Paco. *Why We Buy: The Science of Shopping*. Simon & Schuster, 1990.

Weinreich, Len. *11 Steps to Brand Heaven: The Ultimate Guide to Creating Successful Advertising*. Kogan Page, 2001.

For additional choices, check these Internet sites for advertising and brand-related books.
http://www.Amazon.com—bookstore; click on advertising
http://www.Yahoo.com—search engine; refer to advertising books
http://www.bookwire.com—company site; a source for Web books
http://www.marketingpower.com—company site; a source for marketing books

Book Report Form

Book Title

_____

Author

_____

A. Summarize the main idea of the book here.

B. Describe a memorable incident or interesting concept that impressed you in this book.

C. Relate the contents of this book to what you learned in class or from your text.

D. Would you recommend this book? Why or why not?

Your name_____

SECTION VI
Preparing the Plans Book

Putting It All Together:
Preparing the Plans Book

The Plans Book has two functions in an agency: it acts as a sales tool for the client, and it serves as an agency blue print for the campaign. For your purposes, the Plans Book will demonstrate your ability to research and organize data, to set objectives, to develop specific strategies, and to create effective advertising and promotional tactics.

Below are some key aspects of the Plans Book to guide your preparation.

1. The most important feature of a quality Plans Book is visual appearance. Next is the actual content. Unless the book looks inviting and readable, the client will defer to the presentation. Because the most detailed elements of the plan are contained in the plans book, it's important to make it visually attractive. Use QuarkXPress, PageMaker, or other graphics software to enhance the graphs, charts, and page layouts. Color is suggested

2. Use the meeting planner and Steps 1-10 to write the narrative, as illustrated in the TONI&GUY example. Begin with the situation analysis, which has the most lengthy narrative in the book. The situation analysis establishes common ground between agency and client, articulating a mutual understanding.

3. For the creative, media, and promotions sections, visuals are imperative. The client must be able to see the executions of what the agency has developed. The executions must reflect what was reported in the situation analysis and correspond with the communication objectives.

4. Include an executive summary to explain the contents of the Plans Book. This is written last and summarizes what the plan presents. See an example as presented in the student campaign that follows.

5. Use a spiral binding for the book so it is easily read and referenced. The cover should contain both the agency and brand logos to tie them together.

Student Example

Toni&Guy

Plans Book

The author and Thomson Business & Professional Publishing team are grateful to Toni&Guy for allowing us to publish a student example that draws so heavily on information concerning their company. Please be aware that while Section B, the "Company & Brand History" is accurate, all of the remaining information related to the Toni&Guy scenario is modified or deliberately not accurate for the purposes of creating a fictional ad campaign and student exercise. For those interested in finding out more information concerning the actual company, we suggest you visit their Web site at: http://www.toniguy.com/

EXECUTIVE SUMMARY

This brand communications campaign has as its primary objective to establish Bed Head Boutiques in selected high-end salons in an Orange County, California test market, and to maintain a strong brand awareness of TiGi products among stylists and consumers of hair styling products.

Since its beginning in London, TONI&GUY has expanded to a company with global significance. From its very beginnings, TONI&GUY introduced its Bed Head line to sell only the highest quality hair care products available. Currently, Bed Head is in its growth stage and is continually seeking to maintain a strong connection with salon owners and their stylists.

The Opus Agency™ has developed a comprehensive plan to position Bed Head's products and Boutiques as premiere in the personal care industry.

"What's new today, is old tomorrow and we must keep our brand as fresh and innovative as possible."
Bruno Mascolo, CEO & Chairman, TiGi Worldwide

I. SITUATION ANALYSIS

A. Personal Care Industry

Consumers in the United States spent over $13.8 billion, or about 9 percent of their total spending of $153 billion, on personal care products in 2003. In 2000, the market for personal care and cosmetic products grew 5.7 percent to reach $52.7 billion in retail sales, up from $49.9 billion the previous year. Hair care is a segment of the personal care industry. In 2001, the market for salon hair care products was valued at $210 million, with increasing growth of 34 percent since 1997. Although TONI&GUY is a privately owned company that chooses not to publish company statistics, the hair care industry has revealed that TiGi rates as the Number Three salon brand in the United States. *Salon News*, *Soap & Cosmetics*, and *Soap Perfumery & Cosmetics* as well as *Marketing Week* and *BrandWeek* substantiated basic market revenue data.

B. Company & Brand History

Company Background

From its early development, TONI&GUY established its company by providing only the finest, artistic hairstyling techniques to meet the personal needs of each individual client. In 1963 two Italian-born brothers, Toni and Guy Mascolo, founded TONI&GUY in London, England. Toni and Guy, along with their younger brothers, Anthony and Bruno, operated their company from

The Mascolos': Future hairdressers of Europe and beyond.

one small salon in London, to a second in 1972, and to a third in 1981. TONI&GUY then grew to a million dollar internationally renowned chain of salons located in 12 countries.

Recognized for their "education," "professionalism," and their "seamless service," the brothers opted to franchise their salons in 1988. It was decided to appoint only the highest skilled hairdressers for each particular franchise, who all had at one point already been employed with TONI&GUY. In terms of expression, TONI&GUY deemed itself as "a branded, international franchise of high street hairdressing salons." As it does today, the company strived to deliver "high fashion, well-cut, individual and wearable hairstyles at affordable prices" and in a "family atmosphere."

For the past 40 years, TONI&GUY has achieved a strong, distinctive, and dependable corporate image by providing ongoing education and training for its staff. The TONY&GUY company philosophy stresses positive communication and a powerful sense of visual identity. To accomplish this, TONI&GUY has granted full control to one person, and has also kept close ties between the company and its salons. The TONI&GUY corporate objective is to provide a company community through its quality education for all employees. The TiGi "educational system" is perceived to be the "backbone" of the company to insure high state-of-the-art image, culture, and performance. Staff education and training is completed both at individual salons as well as at the TONI&GUY academies. Each staff member adheres to a prearranged training plan. It takes approximately three years to become a junior stylist. The senior staff and managers participate in training every month, which includes instruction for the hairdressing process, client service, product education, and an expertise in retail.

Furthermore, the staff partake in a quarterly Training Congress, where the most current looks and fashion trends are presented.

To date, TONI&GUY have over 400 salons worldwide, in 20 countries and over 50 salons in the Unites States. Training centers are located in 13 countries, including a traveling art team that visits each location to train staff in the most current haircutting and styling techniques. TONI&GUY has set the mark for all others in the professional hair care industry with annual revenues in excess of $115 million.

Brand Background

To meet the demands of the quality hair care product market, TONI&GUY announced their original TiGiTiGi hair care line in 1984 that would enable customers to maintain their own hairstyles between salon visits.

Founder Bruno Mascolo organized a product line under the TiGi name to avoid confusion with TONY&GUY salons. Vice president of marketing, Kyara Mascolo described Bed Head as a sophisticated line for all ages with insight for each product coming from "teens, musicians, and fashion."

The vast popularity of TiGi brand has earned $300 million in annual revenue, resulting in Bed Head's standing as third largest salon brand in the United States. The company has issued a ten-year, billion-dollar plan for the company. Kyara Mascolo stated the success of Bed Head has been achieved by having a "touch of comedy" while also striving to "push the limits."

Marketing & Mix

For almost a half a century, TONI&GUY has used an innovative marketing mix to develop a strong corporate identity.

Product

Within the Bed Head line, TiGi has tested the limits with racy names and product packaging. Products with names such as Dumb Blonde®, Headbanger®, and Boy Toys® have raised the attention of consumers as well as salons and their stylists. James Morrison, creative director for TONI&GUY salons stated, "It's incredibly popular. It's a way of achieving that separation, that disheveled type of look that everyone wants. Think of Meg Ryan and Hilary Swank." This unique line of products ranges from

ointments to conditioners and is "designed" to make a clean head of hair look completely unwashed. As a result of its mass appeal, TiGi has continuously added new hair care products to the existing line … all aiming to offer hair optimum shine, hold, texture, and volume. The company has transformed itself within the hair care market, branching out to other markets both nationally and globally.

Price

Bed Head's products are considered to be "premium priced". Consumers tend to prefer Bed Head over other brands because of the perceived value from using the product. Products range in price from $7.95–$34.95. According to consumers, product prices are justified by the youthful and vibrant experience not obtainable from any other brand. By buying such a popular brand name in the salon industry, Bed Head consumers are feeding both their physical and emotional needs. As a necessity, many are willing to acquire Bed Head at any cost.

Place

Bed Head is sold in mid- to upper-class neighborhood salons. Distribution links the brand to a sophisticated demographic. In 2000, Bed Head signed a contract with Nordstrom, allowing Bed Head cosmetics to be sold as part of a department store distribution project. With the estimated sale of $2 million dollars for the next year, Bruno Mascolo stated, "The last thing we want to do is to destroy our primary distribution base, which is the salon arena."

Bed Head has been very successful placing its products to appeal to the mass market. Regional manager for trade magazines for the California-based *Modern Salon Media* , Gregg McConnell states, "Bed Head is one of the hottest lines going. It creates a look that hipper people want. It's youth-oriented but not locked to any age group." To cater to such needs while developing their marketing campaign, TiGi has visited the *backstage* of major events in the entertainment industry. This has given them publicity in music, sports, and fashion publications.

Promotion

In 2002, TONI&GUY launched an email-driven marketing campaign that offered new and existing consumers to download coupons from its Web site for discounts on TONI&GUY products. However, the overall advertising strategy has always revolved more on salon promotions and staff training to increase its brand awareness. With this strategy alone, both TONI&GUY and TiGi have developed a brand without having to launch a highly aggressive advertising campaign. The general method of advertising has been placed on print, word of mouth, and more recently, Internet advertising. The current promotional emphasis is through celebrity endorsement. Bed Head recognizes that celebrities set trends by being constantly in the public eye.

The year of 2003 marks the 40th anniversary for TONI&GUY who celebrated their anniversary on May 25th by launching an event at the Grosvenor House Hotel in London.

TONI&GUY hosted the Pure Hair Show in Australia the same year to highlight the latest techniques and styles developed. In April of 2003, TONI&GUY launched their "in house,

worldwide entertainment, and training TV channel," entitled TONI&GUY TV. This cable channel features training videos, presentations on products and stylists as well as music videos.

TiGi provides consistent philanthropic support for breast cancer research During the months of September/October 2003, all proceeds from pink Bed Head products were donated to cancer research. An additional $15,000 donation to the City of Hope supports research and educational efforts.

Technology and Innovation

Bed Head products are developed using experimental testing by laboratory chemists who have been characterized by the salon industry as extreme rule breakers and risk takers when developing product formulas. Feedback comes from salon owners and stylists who help determine whether or not a particular formula should be pursued or eliminated from product development. According to the founder, "Someone would spray something in the air, we'd smell it, and say, 'Yeah let's go with that.'"

TONI&GUY has utilized current technology to market the brand by placing video cameras above stylists' stations to record clients as they are getting their hair styled. With this idea, clients would be able to purchase the tapes and attempt to recreate their hairstyles between salon visits. This technology also enables TONI&GUY to sell and advertise media space on an in-salon TV channel.

In 2000, TONI&GUY created a nationwide appointment-booking database much like the one utilized by the airlines industry. Clients are able to schedule appointments anywhere in the United States over the phone. This database also contains the clients' hair and product history to personalize the needs of individual clients no matter where they are located.

The TONI&GUY Web site also demonstrates the technology and innovation involved with their branding techniques. In 2002, TONI&GUY signed on with SMS marketing to

offer interactive marketing incentives like "subscription services, personalized contacts, e-zines, and promotions." Through such a Web site, TONI&GUY is able to develop close ties with their clients to better understand their personal needs. Alex Michael, managing director for all of TONI&GUY's digital technology, believes that the TiGi list, which is a combinations of cellphone numbers and e-mail addresses, is an important part of the marketing mix.

Legal & Political Influences

Throughout the years, TiGi has discovered counterfeit products placed in a variety of stores and outlet centers throughout the United States and in Canada. Bed Head products are being been distributed and sold illegally, which jeopardizes the business of TiGi as well as their established relationship with TONI&GUY. To monitor such illegal activity, TiGi hired a former CIA agent whose sole function is to track down offenders. In a joint venture, TiGi filed a federal lawsuit in January of 2003 with the U. S. Postal Inspectors, Health Canada, U.S.

Customs, and the Food & Drug Administration. Several counterfeited products have been seized and injunctions have been filed though the court system.

Environmental Concerns

Although entertaining, TiGi's product packaging is neither recyclable nor reusable. The product image is built on visual identity and physical differentiation from other brands. TiGi performs its product testing on human hair and does not participate in animal testing.

Social Trends

Hair Idols

As with TONI&GUY salons, TiGi has been formulated for use by both female and male consumers. Over the past several years, there has been more of a need for "guy-friendly" hair care products as studies have concluded that men are coloring and styling their hair more than ever. TiGi has observed this trend, and has developed products within their Bed Head line that appeal especially to men. Hair gel and creams such as Bed Head Manipulator® and Bed Head Power Trip® are just some of the few that have grown in popularity with men since their launch. Bed Head line has been continually successful with female consumers. Research has proven that women's attraction to high-style fashion and their connection with magazines such as *Cosmopolitan* and *Vogue* have led to an easy relationship with the hottest trends and the use of the Bed Head product line.

Celebrities have a substantial influence over current fashion trends in both hair and apparel. Consumers choose to use Bed Head because its association with celebrities and the entertainment industry. Using the same hair care products as prominent public figures is a way for the average consumer elevate his or her social status.

Economic Influence

With a wavering economy, consumers may be more inclined to spend less money than when employment rates are higher. But because Bed Head and TONI&GUY feed an emotional and physical need, consumers still purchase and use their favorite hair brand. Consumers feel that they deserve to use such a high quality products. TONI&GUY consumers are brand conscious and will use products less frequently rather than switch to a lower priced brand or salon.

C. Product Evaluation

Bruno and Kyara Mascolo

TONI&GUY currently manufacture six product lines— *TiGi, TiGi Classics, Bed Head, Catwalk, Unleashed and Hardcore.* Each individual product line is distinct in its own right. Five different TiGi product lines include *TiGi Classics, Bed Head, Catwalk, Unleashed and Hardcore*—Bed Head has proven to be the most popular, growing from 70 to 100 percent annually since it was launched in 1997. Presently, the Bed Head line includes 33 hair care products and has expanded to skin care and a line of cosmetics.

- **Product strengths** lie in their cheeky names and functions. After Party, Boy Toys, Control Freak, Chocolate Head, Dumb Blonde, Ego Boost, Girl Toys, Hard Head, Head Banger, Headrush, Head Shrink, Health Goddess, Manipulator, Mastermind Bite Me! Hair Candy, Maxxed Out, Power Trip, Rubber Rage, Shine Junkie, Small Talk, and Uptight are among the most popular products.

- **Product weaknesses** include non-environmental packaging and higher prices than the competition.

D. Competitive Analysis

There are many hair care products on the market, but Bed Head's main competitors are Bumble & Bumble, Aveda, and Paul Mitchell. Because Paul Mitchell is marketed to a different consumer segment, they are not included in our competitive evaluation. In a price comparison of

100

the six leading hair care product lines, Bed Head prices fall between the mid- to high-price range. The cleaning products fall to the mid-to-low price range with the styling products averaging as the most expensive.

The chart on the next page highlights product differences.

Both Aveda and Bumble & Bumble have a network of elite salons, which carry their exclusive product line. Aveda hair care products offer the benefits of natural ingredients and environmental responsibility as well as a holistic feeling of being able to enhance beauty without using harsh chemicals. Aveda believes that their products treat users with care and respect.

Bumble and bumble.
NEW YORK

Bumble & Bumble has a similar approach to cutting edge style of fashion and hairdressing especially by the use of targeting models and celebrities as Bed Head.

Analysis of Promotional Efforts

Aveda promotes through a Web site and within their own retail locations. Their stores' spa ambiance lures consumers with aromatic mood-lifting fragrances that bestow a sense of well-being by merely using the product. This continues to build on the connection of nature to the product. Aveda also promotes through their institutes and concept schools, instructing and inspiring stylists to excel in their careers and to promote products that are environmentally friendly.

Hair Care Price Comparison

	Bed Head		Bumble and Bumble		Aveda	
	Product Name	Sug. Retail	Product Name	Retail	Product Name	Sug. Retail
Shampoo & Conditioner						
	Control Freak Shampoo (defrizz) (12oz)	$ 7.95	Alojoba Shampoo (light-weight, moisture)	$ 18.00	Shampure Shampoo (daily) (8.5 oz)	$ 11.99
	Control Freak Conditioner (defrizz) (8.5oz)	$ 11.95	Alojoba Conditioner (light-weight, moisture)	$ 18.00	Shampure Conditioner (daily) (8.5 oz)	$ 9.99
	Manipulator Shampoo (body and texture)	$ 8.95	Seaweed Shampoo (mild, moisturizing, shine)	$ 13.00	Sap Moss Shampoo (nourishing, for dry hair) (4.2oz)	$ 14.99
	Manipulator Conditioner (detangler, strength)	$ 11.95	Super Rich Conditioner (for all hair types, color-treated)	$ 18.00	Sap Moss Conditioning Detangler (4.2oz)	$ 11.00
	Dumb Blonde Shampoo (colored hair) (12oz)	$ 9.95	Thickening Shampoo (fine, seal split ends, smooths)	$ 17.00	Color Conserve Shampoo (color-treated) (8.5oz)	$ 12.00
	Dumb Blonde Reconstructor (colored hair) (6oz)	$ 15.95	Thickening Conditioner (fuller effect)	$ 18.00	Color Conserve Conditioner (color-treated) (6.7oz)	$ 12.00
Styling products						
	Headbanger (texturize)	$ 18.95	Styling Lotion (fine hair, body, shine, soft hold)	$ 19.00	Brilliant Forming Gel (5 oz)	$ 15.00
	Manipulator (texturize)	$ 16.95	Thickening Spray (body, defrizz)		Flax Seed/Aloe Strong Hold Sculpting Gel (8.5oz)	$ 11.00
	Rubber Rage (texturize)	$ 18.50	Styling Crème (body, control)	$ 19.00	Hang Straight Straightening Lotion (6.7oz)	$ 16.00
	Creative Genius (sculpting liquid)	$ 13.95	Grooming Crème (texture, hold, smooth)	$ 21.00	Light Elements Smoothing Fluid (3.4oz)	$ 23.00
	Head Shrink (firm gel) (8.5oz)	$ 11.95	Brilliantine (texture, shine)	$ 16.00	Self Control Hair Styling Stick (2.5oz)	$ 15.50
	After-Party (smoothing cream)	$ 17.95	Styling Wax (texture, hold)	$ 16.00	Control Paste (1.7oz)	$ 21.00
	Girl Toys (shine serum)	$ 16.50	Sumowax (hard wax, define texture, hold, shine)	$ 20.00		
			Defrizz (smooths)	$ 19.00		
			Straight (curly hair smooth)	$ 21.00		
			Gloss (shine)	$ 14.00		

Bumble & Bumble has a slightly different approach: they promote from within salons, movie studios, and runway fashion. They also create classrooms with laboratories for stylists to get educated in the development of their products from high-end fashion models to the average person. They promote with magazines, fashion shows, celebrities, and stylists. Both Bumble & Bumble and Aveda have already introduced an exclusive network of elite salons that are the exclusive retailers of the companies' complete hair care product lines.

Strengths and Weakness

AVEDA

- Aveda's **strengths** are primarily focused on lifestyle and how the consumer is able to give back to the environment. This allows their products to encompass part of nature's cycle since they are made of natural ingredients.

- Aveda's main **weakness** is its conservative product packaging and marketing. Aveda does not demonstrate an interest in the fashion industry and prefers to promote through its own retail outlets.

BUMBLE AND BUMBLE

- Bumble & Bumble **strengths** are remaining current on the latest fashions and hairstyles as well as a consistency of focus on their selected target audience. They place their products at events and trade shows and stay current with the latest trends and styles.

- Their **weakness** is uncreative product names and packaging. Containers are bare and monotonous product names are plain and modest.

E. Consumer Evaluation

Primary Research Method

The Opus Agency's™ primary research was conducted using a questionnaire with fifty consumers, five salon owners and five stylists. Primary research revealed a better and more thorough understanding of Bed Head consumers and their personal experiences, associations, and perceptions of the brand and its products.

Data Analysis

Salon Owners

The results of the questionnaire given to salon owners revealed that when selecting products for their salons, they chose products that were in high demand and were good sellers. However, salon owners considered quality and a good industry reputation more important than sales. Most of those interviewed seemed to believe that the products they carry reflect the type of salon they are: An exclusive salon carries only exclusive lines that reflect the very best image.

Top-of-mind association of the Bed Head brand by salon owners was high. The brand perceptions and image carry a positive tone with nearly all of the salon owners interviewed. Specifically, fun and outrageous lifestyles were two attributes associated with the brand. Moreover, most salon owners felt that these associations carried over into their salon environment and image.

Stylist

Salon stylists are conscientious about the products they recommend to clients and are extremely brand loyal. Overall, these products must be of top quality and they should also provide value, but they place a premium on the performance of the product. It must consistently perform with great results.

User Satisfaction

According to survey results, Bed Head products have high user satisfaction. Consumers enjoy the product because of what it does for their hair as well as the "cool" appeal. Typically a stylist introduces the Bed Head products to the client. The stylist uses it on the client's hair and the client then buys more products because of the great results. Users find the product to be of good quality, and it doesn't hurt that the image is also humorous, funky, and sexy.

Secondary Research Insights to Salon Owner and Stylist Target Market

What do Britney Spears and Marilyn Manson have in common? Both are celebrities and enjoy the irreverent brand named Bed Head. Britney dabbles with Dumb Blonde®, a

shampoo and conditioner product. Manson rocks out with the Manipulator®, a product that makes your hair stand on end. As much as we love celebrities, they are not the prototypical consumer of TONI&GUY for this campaign. In fact, the primary consumers for this campaign are owners of high-end salons.

A recent study conducted by the National Accrediting Commission of Cosmetology Arts and Sciences (NACCAS) on job demand randomly sampled 6,177 salons in the nation. 70,000 surveys were mailed to salon owners asking about the previous year (2002) as well as future trends. The key findings concluded, "The typical salon is a small full service salon with five stations, three full-time professionals and two part-time professionals. Salon owners report an average of 155 clients per week. The research also concluded there has been "notable growth in the industry since 1999." In the industry, almost 60 percent of salon owners classify themselves as full service, 18 percent as haircutting salons, 4 percent as nail salons, and 5 percent are considered barbershops. NACCAS also reports that there is "a crisis to find qualified salon professions as American consumer's needs and demands rapidly rise for professional image-oriented and relaxing hair, skin, nail and spa services ... from Generation Next Teens to the aging Baby Boomers and beyond, everyone wants to look and feel

their best today." Why is this important, you might ask? It shows the possible advantage of a strategic alliance with TONI&GUY. According to *Salon News* in an article titled, "Young at heart", the next generation of salon owners are under thirty, goal-oriented, and achieve their entrepreneurial goals very early in life.

TONI&GUY as a brand works. It sells itself. Behind The Chair (http://www.behindthechair.com), a Web site focused to the cosmetologist and salon professional, provided oodles of insights that are relevant for marketing new TONI&GUY Boutique concept:

"If a 45 year old or 55 year old or 60 year old walks in here, we're going to make her happy. TONI&GUY is not just for young people. Here we will prove that we can please everyone."   - Guy Mascolo

"Our clientele covers a wide variety of ages, hair textures and lengths. Most important is to keep you and your clientele constantly talking about what's new/fresh in hair, so nobody gets stale."
     - James Morrison

An intriguing potential consumer is the "Metrosexual, who, according to Wordsmith.com, is a dandyish narcissist in love with not only himself, but also his urban lifestyle; a straight man who is in touch with his feminine side. Men who aren't afraid to look good, smell good, and feel good. "Men—of all sexualities—are taking a greater interest in their appearance. They go to hairdressers rather than barbers … straight men are … changing because women demand their partners take greater effort with their appearance … appearance and grooming are really important.

SWOT Analysis

Strengths

- TONI&GUY is an international company that offers high quality products and is at the forefront of creative hairstyles. They are family owned with a forty-year history. Today, TONI&GUY has over 400 salons worldwide, and has educational centers throughout the U.S., Europe, Australia, and several Asian countries. In terms of product recognition, TiGi products are the third most recognizable brand name of all salon brands in the United States.

- High brand recognition among consumers
- Brand equity with salon owners and stylists
- Educational focus with Academies located throughout the world

Weaknesses

- The hair care market is becoming increasingly more competitive due to the large number of outlets selling hair care products.
- Major supermarkets are expanding their hair care ranges and retailers are devoting additional space to hair care.
- Women prefer to purchase hair products from mass-market outlets, which run promotional campaigns on the hair salon brands that are more expensive at the salon.

- Shampoo is the only product of any significance purchased by women from hair salons.

- There is a tendency to believe there is no difference in quality between salon products and standard products.

- The emergence of designer hair care brands stocked by mass-market retailers causes confusion among consumers.

- A majority of men are still unwilling to leave the local barbershop and go to a hair salon.

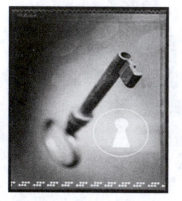

Opportunities

Sales of salon brand products tend to be influenced by factors including changing demographics, hairdressers, and brand awareness. Manufacturers of salon products have decided that their future success relies on reaching younger consumers who tend to be more adventurous when it comes to new hairstyles. Salons located in trendy shopping malls may be the best way to reach this valuable group. Research suggests that salon choice among this group is primarily based on their impression of the stylists who work in the salon. "If the stylists are wearing trendy hairstyles that I would like to wear, I know that this is the place for me."

- Because of older women's propensity to visit salons more frequently for coloring and cutting, they represent a strong opportunity for professional salon brands. One of the main reasons for this opportunity is that their numbers are growing as a proportion of the overall population. Furthermore, with the number of women aged 35 and over set to increase substantially over the next few years, manufacturers of salon products need to take their changing hair care needs into account by producing relevant products. Specifically, hair care producers should develop shampoos and conditioners, which target hair problems encountered during menopause.

- Men's growing interest in grooming as a whole has created a niche market not previously available to hair salons. Although many men are still reluctant to switch from a barbershop to a hair salon, some salons are successfully luring men by creating environments specifically targeted at them..

- Currently, there is a tendency to believe there is no difference in quality between salon products and standards Bed Head has an opportunity to educate consumers of the benefits of salon products.

- Research suggests consumer demand for branded salon products will promote steady growth in that sector up to 2006. Consumer spending on personal grooming products, especially on designer hair care brands will see an increase in growth of approximately 24 percent. The role of the hair salon will be crucial to this continued growth, both in terms of promoting the products and providing advice to customers.

- With consumers attempting to copy fashion-oriented styles seen in popular media, styling aids are set to remain the largest sector of the personal care/salon product market. With the overall increase in interest in personal grooming and hair salon products, hair salons will benefit from offering advice and encouraging consumers to buy on impulse. Bed Head has an opportunity to provide incentives for stylists to recommend its products on a large scale.

Threats

According to a recent report by *Mintel*, the hair care market has seen significant changes in the last couple of years. Professional hair care brands have maintained a strong point of difference. However, the emergence of salon hair care brands stocked by mass-market retailers has caused confusion among consumers who expect to buy hair care products in salons and not in the retail environment.

- Many premium salon brands stocked by mass-market retailers are counterfeits. Currently, there is much litigation regarding this matter. As of yet, nothing has been resolved. The greatest threat from counterfeit products is that premium brands risk loosing precious brand equity that is critical for future success.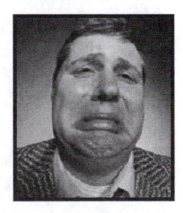

- With the influx of many new personal care products, manufactures of salon brands must adhere to the CANI business principle: Constant and Never-Ending Improvement. Salon owners must continuously look for ways to keep their brands relevant to their consumers' needs.

Table O' SWOT	
Strengths - high brand equity/recognition - strong consumer loyalty - competitive price structure - image drive/interpreter of fashion - edgy but still sophisticated - celebrity endorsed - rock star image - growing popularity of hairstylist - public's interest in celebrity styles - constantly evolving and improving business - T&G ensures good service levels - ongoing training/education and product knowledge - strict code of business ethics and philosophies - strong presence in the personal care industry - franchise ownership requires extensive training - brand extensions: Essensuals, next generation of salons; Catwalk exclusive product line; TiGi - increasingly growing market - growth of online shopping - products designed by hairdressers for hairdressers	**Weaknesses** - part of an oversaturated market - limited or no information regarding company - Web site lacks creativity found in their products - hairstylist not motivated to promote products - not much differentiation among competitors - limited locations equates to lower product recognition - prohibitive price - no specific point of difference between salon brands and retail brands - need to create welcoming environments for men - increase in product purchases from unlicensed distributors
Opportunities - younger consumers tend to spend more on salon products: more disposable income - women aged 35 and over set to increase substantially over the next few years: visit salons more frequently for coloring and cutting - salon products need to take their changing hair care needs into account by producing relevant products. - men's growing interest in grooming as a whole has created a niche market not previously available to hair salons - hairdressers are in a strong position to support products sold in their salons - stylists need to be offered attractive financial incentives to sell salon products - salon users willing to pay a premium for salon products - salon brands need to increase education to differentiate themselves from mass-marketed products - consumers spending on personal grooming products, especially designer hair care brands will see an increase in growth of approximately 24 percent - styling aids are set to remain the largest sector of the personal care/salon product market - conditioners are expected to show growth of 45 percent - celebrities sell products, so salon brands should sponsor more celebrities - promotions, i.e., as offering two hair care products at a reduced price should encourage consumers to purchase salon brand	**Threats** - confusion among consumers - counterfeits - legal issues and copyright infringement - not being relevant to consumers' needs - not looking for innovative ways to deliver better quality products - not staying competitive - voice in market drowned out by competitors

III. GOALS & OBJECTIVES

A. Marketing Objectives

Sales

The Opus Agency's™ campaign goal is to make a local impact in the Orange County, California test market acquiring 25 percent of TiGi salons for boutique associations.

Orange County is the perfect test market due to its high income, image conscientiousness, and purchase driven consumers. Orange County is known for its diversity in both income levels and the "OC" trend influence.

The Bed Head Boutique concept should synergistically feed off the brand's success, the need for constantly improved products, and flexibility. The boutique concept will be in Orange County's elite salons, and exposure of the Bed Head Boutique concept will lead consumers to patronize these salons and embrace new product lines. The Boutique will satisfy the salon owners' need for exclusivity and add to the overall cachet of TiGi.

Market Share

We will increase TiGi's market share by 10 percent within the 2004 fiscal year. The Opus Agency's ™ two-year plan forecasts Bed Head as aggressively competing with the number one brand in 2005.

2003 Estimate

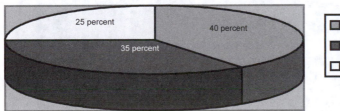

- □ B & B
- ■ Aveda
- □ Bed Head

B. Communications Objectives

Category Need

This campaign will create the need for Bed Head Boutiques among 20 percent of salon owners in our test market area within one year.

Awareness

The campaign will create a 90 percent recall awareness of the Bed Head Boutique concept among salon owners and stylists in the test market within one year.

Attitude

The campaign will create excitement about the concept of Bed Head's Boutique among salon owners and develop a positive attitude about Bed Head products among stylists.

Purchase Intention

The campaign will create purchase intention for the Bed Head Boutique concept among salon owners in our test market area.

IV. BUDGET

The Opus Agency™ has elected the overall campaign budget to be comprised of three separate entities: Media, Promotions, and Public Relations. The majority of the expenses fall under Media and Promotions. Media is given 40 percent (approximately $80,000); Promotions, 50 percent (approximately $100,000); and Public Relations, 10 percent (approximately $20,000) of the $200,000 overall budget. The rationale of this decision is based on The Opus Agency's™ recognition to launch an intense campaign to properly introduce the new Bed Head Boutique concept.

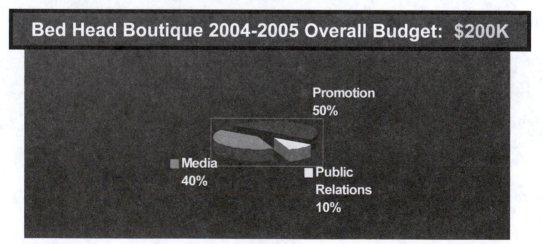

Bed Head Boutique 2004-2005 Overall Budget: $200K

Promotion 50%

Media 40%

Public Relations 10%

Media Budget

A media budget of $80,000 consists of trade publication advertisements and updating the Bed Head Web site on the Internet.

Promotion Budget

The magic happens in the promotion budget. The Opus Agency™ strongly believes that establishing personal connections and relationships with targeted high-end salons is crucial. To accomplish this goal, the majority of the overall budget is devoted to establishing and maintaining awareness of the new boutique concept through channels of promotions. One of the means of promotions includes event sponsorship (50 percent of the promotion budget), which consists of trade shows and an outrageous "out of the box" Bed Head Boutique launch event to be discussed in detail in section VII. Twenty percent of the promotion budget translates to $20,000, which will cover the reproduction/printing costs of all of collaterals (brochures).

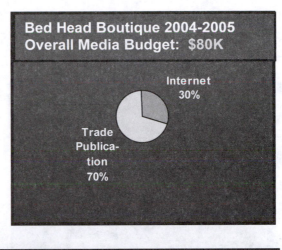

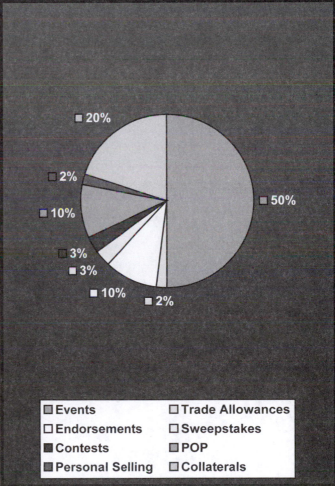

Furthermore, ten thousand dollars will be set aside for "endorsements." These endorsements tie in to event sponsorship and trade shows therefore less emphasis will be placed in public relations. Due to the relatively low investment, both sweepstakes and contests will be weighted at 3 percent each and point-of-purchase will be allocated at $10,000. The remainder of the promotion budget will be assigned to personal selling

113

at 2 percent, and trade allowances at $2,000. The budget for personal selling will cover the costs involved in salon demonstrations and training sessions.

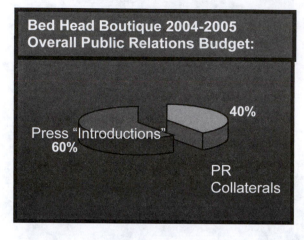

Public Relations Budget

The Opus Agency's ™ public relations budget of $20,000 includes a press kit and a variety of press releases to create a sense of excitement about the Bed Head Boutique concept. $12,000 will be allocated to introducing the press to the Bed Head Boutique through products, demonstrations and events.

V. CREATIVE BRIEF

For Salon Owners	For Salon Stylists

What is the opportunity and/or problem the advertising must address?

Opportunities	Opportunities
▪ Exclusivity ▪ Expansion	▪ Build recommendations ▪ Create relationship

What do we want to do as a result of the advertising?

Create Desire to purchase boutique	Image Enhancement and attitude maintenance

Who are we talking about?

Salon Owners	Salon Stylists
▪ In high-end Orange County salons ▪ Entrepreneur spirit ▪ Adventurous and savvy	▪ Skewed towards female ▪ Youth-orientated/Trendy ▪ Different/ "exotic"

What is the key response we want?

Boutique Investment and loyalty	Brand Loyalty, Referral

What information/attributes might help produce this response?

Opens Doors For Profits	Brand Fulfillment
▪ Co-op ▪ Free advertising/promotion ▪ Training/Education	▪ Quality ▪ Liability ▪ Consistency

What aspect of brand personality should advertising express?

Quality	Fashion Statement

Are there media or budget considerations?

No Media Considerations	Promotions Product Incentives
▪ $ 5k Investment ▪ Free Salon/Co-op Ads	▪ Coupons ▪ Samples ▪ Brochures

What other information might affect the creative direction?

▪ The Economy/Budget Constraints ▪ Counterfeit Products	N/A

Boutique Info:

1.800.BED.HEAD
WWW.tigiboutique.com

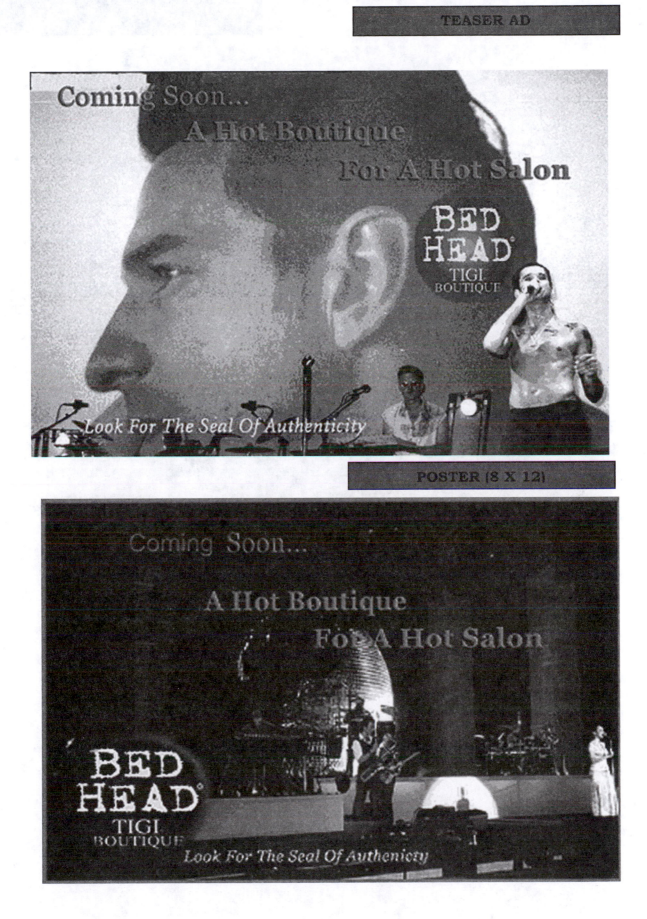

POSTER (8 X 12)

117

118

VI. MEDIA PLAN

A. Media Objectives

Continuity

The Opus Agency™ suggests a *flighting* pattern due to the seasonality of trade shows and client repurchasing cycle. Bed Head may capitalize on their advertising during the periods that best meet the product sales which will also act as a budget check function between advertising efforts to save money.

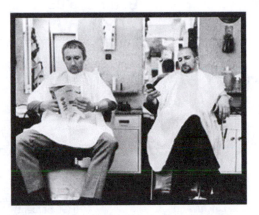

Reach

The Opus Agency™ suggests advertising for the Bed Head Boutique will obtain an average of 90 percent of its Orange County test market in the first month. When the desired *reach* is met, Bed Head will sustain optimum brand awareness of the new boutique concept.

Frequency

An average *frequency* of 4 will maximize the efforts of the advertisers and meet the numbers necessary to create a state of action on the salon owner's behalf.

Bed Head Boutique 2004–2005 Media Objectives

Time Period	Reach	Frequency	GRP's
1. Apr/May	Hi (90 percent)	Low (4)	720
2. Jun/Jul/ Aug/	Hi (90 percent)	Med (5)	450
3. Sept/Oct	Hi (90 percent)	Low (4)	720
4. Nov	--	--	--
5. Dec/Jan	Hi (90 percent)	Med (5)	450
6. Feb/Mar	--	--	

Campaign R/F Average 60/80 percent   4/5   **Total**
GRP's = 2,340

Bed Head Boutique 2005–2006 Media Objectives

Time Period	Reach	Frequency	GRP's
1. Jan 450	Hi (90 percent)	Med (5)	
2. Feb/Mar	--	--	--
3. Apr/May 720	Hi (90 percent)	Low (4)	
3. Jun/Jul/Aug 450	Hi (90 percent)	Med (5)	
4. Sept/Oct 720	Hi (90 percent)	Low (4)	
5. Nov	--	--	--
6. Dec	Hi (90 percent)	Med (5)	450
Campaign R/F Average GRP's = 2,790	68/90 percent	4/5	**Total**

B. Media Strategy

Target

The scope for the Bed Head Boutique concept is narrowly defined in terms of "geodemographics": high-end salon owners in Orange County, California. In theory, the target market consists of approximately 50 salon owners who have been pre-selected by TiGi. For a successful campaign, TiGi's goal is to have a strategic alliance with a minimum of 10 salons in the local region. Contingent with the success of this test market, a national campaign will be implemented.

Media Classes

Both *Soap & Cosmetics* and *Salon News* have been selected as the best possible choices to reach the selected target audience. Television, radio and outdoor advertisements were omitted because size of the test market as well as the high cost of exposure. The agency's decision to utilize the Internet as a non-traditional media was based on the high involvement of the boutique and the available technology to promote each individual salon. Internet media will consist of online banners and a virtual Bed Head Boutique and will assist with the overall objective in maximizing the reach and frequency. Thus, Internet media will be executing a variety of advertisements promoting the Bed Head Boutique and the participating VIP locations. Altogether, this information will be posted on the TiGi, TONI&GUY, and virtual Boutique Web sites. Through these channels an interactive site will enable salons to view information and images on the latest Bed Head products and with information on how they can become part of the Bed Head family. With such a small target audience it is feasible to personally tailor a message utilizing the Internet to local salon owners of what the "hot" new salon concept is in their local area.

. **Bed Head Boutique 2004-2005 Media Launch Schedule Budget:**

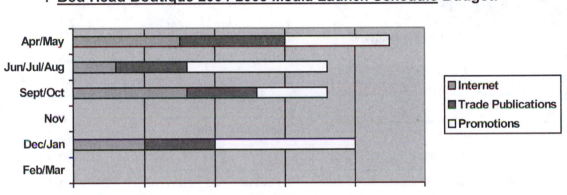

Bed Head Boutique 2005-2006 Media Schedule

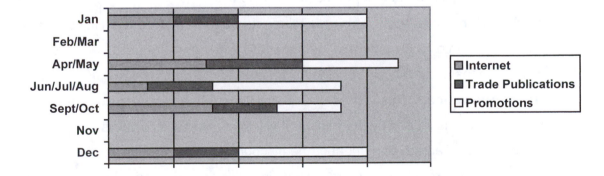

VII. SALES PROMOTION RECOMMENDATIONS

Sales Promotion (Trade)

In order to retain and expand Bed Head's presence in Orange County's most elite salons, particularly the ten preferred salons, a sales promotion plan has be created by The Opus Agency™ to entice the salon owners to carry the new boutique. With this in mind, the agency has set objectives to effectively introduce the Bed Head Boutique concept to salons, increase product distribution, build inventory and increase and expand boutique space. The main messages that will be conveyed are the features and benefits that the new boutique will provide which will lead to an increase in salon traffic. The sales promotional plan will include the following items:

- **Authentic Retail Sign:** This authentic VIP sign for each participating salon will encourage Bed Head consumers to validate the salon's VIP status on TiGi Web site.

- **Announcement Sign:** Prior to the installation of the boutique in each salon, will be a sign on the existing Bed Head shelves that will announce the new products that will be appearing at that particular VIP salon.

- **Product Demonstration:** This will include an appearance from a TiGi educator who comes into each salon to demonstrate the new product's features and benefits to the salon owners and their stylists.

- **Trade Allowance:** This will be a 2 percent per-case rebate paid to retailers when an order is placed by their salon. It will also give salon owners 2 percent of the total cost of an advertisement or the discounted price.

- **Recessed Impression:** A recessed impression on Bed Head's product packaging, either on the base or lid of the product, will protect against counterfeiting and reassure the salon owners that Bed Head is a high-end and desirable product.

- **Salon/Stylist Training:** If the salons purchase a certain amount of product, they will receive a 20 percent off cutting/coloring session with TONI&GUY for a selected stylist in their salon. The salon will also receive a window display stating that this VIP salon offers professionally trained Bed Head stylists.
Other sales promotion activities will be sweepstakes, contests, trade shows, and an event target to the salon owners and the their stylists.

- **Sweepstakes:** A sweepstakes entry form is provided on flyers and brochures to be handed out at trade shows; winners will be announced on the TiGi Web site and newsletter.

- **Contest:** TiGi will also host the "Edgiest New Look of 2004" contest by using new Bed Head boutique products. The stylists will have the opportunity to take down the products names demonstrated and how they are applied. They will also be given a photograph of the finished hairstyle and will have a chance to win hair cutting/coloring training and products.

- **Trade Shows:** TiGi will also host a booth in a high traffic area within the trade show floor. The booth will have the Bed Head Boutique display filled with the new product line. They will provide goody bags with t-shirts, product samples, coupons and TiGi newsletters. There will be a drawing for a complete hair care line (shampoo, conditioner and two styling products) or training at the TiGi School of Hair Care. All contact information obtained from the drawing will be added to the TiGi database.

- **Event:** There will also be a launch party for the Bed Head Boutique concept, which will be in collaboration with the *House of Blues* in Anaheim in May of 2004. This idea will promote a backstage vibe at an exclusive event using bands associated with Bed Head. Such bands might include: *The*

Donnas, *Foo Fighters*, or *Audioslave*. Local bands such as *Good Charlotte*, *Dashboard Confessional*, or *Simple Plan* will be featured as well. Naturally, the *real* star of the event would be the Bead Head POP display shining in the middle of the stage. The host of the event will be a popular Bed Head lover Ryan Seacrest. Using radio, we will promote the *House of Blues/Bed Head Boutique* launch party on the air with free tickets to the event for listeners.

VIII. PUBLIC RELATIONS RECOMMENDATIONS

Press coverage will be available through interviews on local cable talk shows, press releases, and a press kit. News releases will be sent to announce the following:

- House of Blues/Bed Head Boutique launch event and co-sponsorship in May of 2004. Information will be delivered to editors of specific sections of *The Los Angeles Times*, *The Orange County Register* plus trade publications.

- Bed Head Boutique showcase at the 2004 Spectrum Beauty Expo in Los Angeles, CA and at the International Salon and Spa Expo in Long Beach, CA, and other top tradeshows in Southern California.

- The status of court cases regarding counterfeit TiGi products, and how a salon/stylists can verify that their products are legitimate.

- "Edgiest New Look" of 2004 contest. **Los Angeles Times**

Bed Head press kits will be personally delivered to the local newspapers including *The Orange County Register* and *The Los Angeles Times*. These press kits will include story ideas, biographies of corporate executives. and fact sheets.

IX. DATABASE MARKETING RECOMMENDATIONS

In addition to TONI&GUY's current consumer marketing database, the Bed Head Boutique will formulate a similar database to keep record of prospective salon owners and their stylists. All contact information for the database will be obtained from trade show participants who have registered their salon either by business card or entry form. TiGi will select an assortment of Orange County salons (owners/stylists) to be invited to the Bed Head Boutique launch party at the Anaheim House of Blues.

X. CAMPAIGN EVALUATION

Within the first year of the launch, The Opus Agency™ will measure the success of the campaign primarily by assessing the "buy-in" of the number of the boutiques sold to salon owners. Other measures include:

- Web site hits, promotional responses and trade show attendance.

- Pre- and post-tests levels of awareness, attitude and purchase intention objectives, which will be monitored on a monthly basis.

- Scanner data for product sales increases.

XI. REFERENCES

1. A Really Bad Hair Day; Counterfeit Shampoos Poses Contamination Threat. *The Daily Herald –Tribune* (May 23, 2003): 22.
2. Bed Head Headbanger. *Cosmetics International Cosmetic Products Report* (March 2002) 17, no. 206: 2.
3. Cosmetology Job Demand Research Report. *The Yearbook of Experts, Authorities and Spokespersons* (Sept. 15, 2003).
4. Clark, Mairi. An Experts View. *Strada (*July 6, 2001):14.
5. Discussions in Link with TONI&GUY For Bath Range. *Promotions & Incentives* (November 20, 2002): 4.
6. Dwek, Robert. TONI&GUY*. Marketing Week* (January 17, 2002): 15.
7. Frederic, Fekkai. *TONI&GUY & Vidal Sassoon.*
8. Hair Care with Rare Flair. *The Express* (London, July 22, 2002):51.
9. Hair Fusion. *Salon News* (January 2002): 67.
10. Hall, Cheryl. News Ideas At Work Column. *Knight Ridder/Tribune Business News.* TiGi Has Teamed Up Its Bed Head Wax Stick and Rubber Rage. *Cosmetics International Cosmetic Products Report (*May 2002;): 4.
11. Health and Beauty Mart Follows Hot Trends. *Chemical Week International (*May 7, 2003): 21–22.
12. Madison Men: TONI&GUY Bite the Big Apple. http://www.behindthechair.com.
13. Management Today: Toni Mascolo—TONI&GUY*; Knight Ridder/Tribune Business News* (July 2001): 78.
14. TONI&GUY Launches In-Store TV Service. *Marketing* (July 11, 2002): 6.
15. Melaniphy, Margie. Young At Heart. *Salon News* (January 2002): 14.
16. Naughton, Julie. TONI&GUY's New Retailing Rack. *WWD* (August 4, 2000): 7.
17. Nelson, Emily. Beauty, Beast: Cosmetics Companies Are Starting to Go Where the Boys Are—They Aim Soap, Dyes at Guys, But Are Quick to Lose the "Pouf." *The Asian Wall Street Journal* (August 11, 2000): 1.
18. On the Cutting Edge. *The Business Journal* (December 8, 2000): 33.
19. Product Focus. *Salon News* (January 2000): 24.
20. Ross, Nicole. A TONI Neighborhood. *Salon News* (June 2000): 56.
21. Schoolcraft, Lisa. Goody's Loses Lawsuit Over Phony T-Shirts. *Atlanta Business Chronicle (*July 9, 2003).
22. Simpson, Mark. Meet the Metrosexual. http://www.salon.com. Superstar Styling. *European Cosmetic Markets*(January 2003): 33. http://www.behindthechair.com/content/212/stylin_la.asp. September 1, 2002.
23. Takahama, Valerie. Dirty Tricks: A New Family of Hair Products Are Designed To Make Clean Hair Look Dirty. *The Orange County Register* (June 19, 2002): E01.
24. Trend Spotting—Beauty Salons Transitioning. *Delaney Report* (November 20, 2002): 11–14.
25. TONI&GUY (Marketing*). Brand Strategy* (July 22, 2002): 5. TONI&GUY Uses Freeport Edge To Boost Distribution. *The Dallas Business Journal* (February 2, 2001): 7.
26. TONI&GUY Takes Italy By Storm. *Drug &Cosmetic Industry* (April 1998): 14.
27. TONI&GUY Launches Site *New Media Age* (December 20, 2001): 2.
28. Toni & Guy Embraces E-Marketing Strategy in First Wave of Web Blitz. *Precision Marketing* (January 11, 2002).
29. TONI&GUY Trials SMS Promotion. *Revolution* (January 9, 2002): 8.
30. TiGi Has Added a Number of New Products to Its Bed Head Range Including Unisex Hair Wax, Boy Toys. *Soap, Perfumery & Cosmetics Asia* (March 2003): 7.

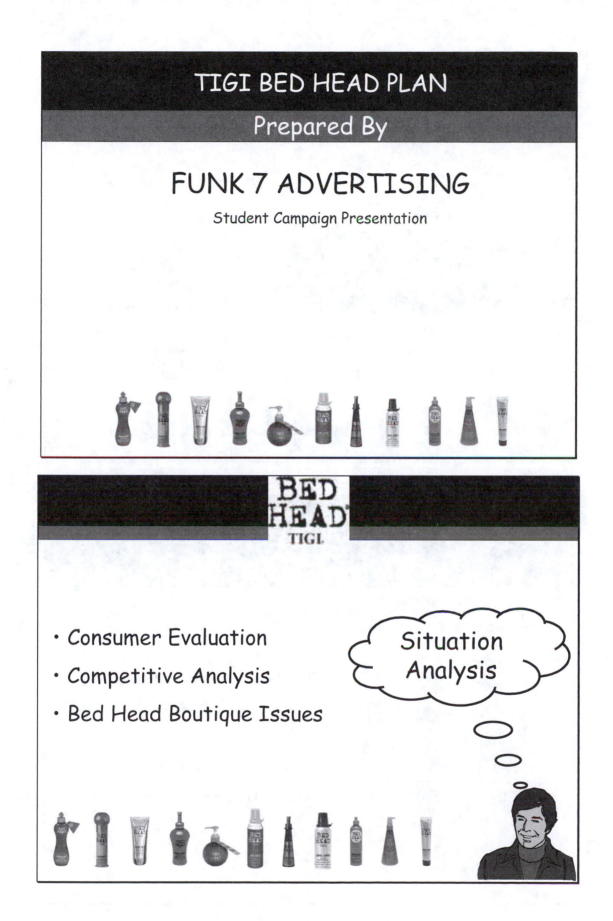

ONE-YEAR ADVERTISING BUDGET
TIGI Bed Head Boutiques

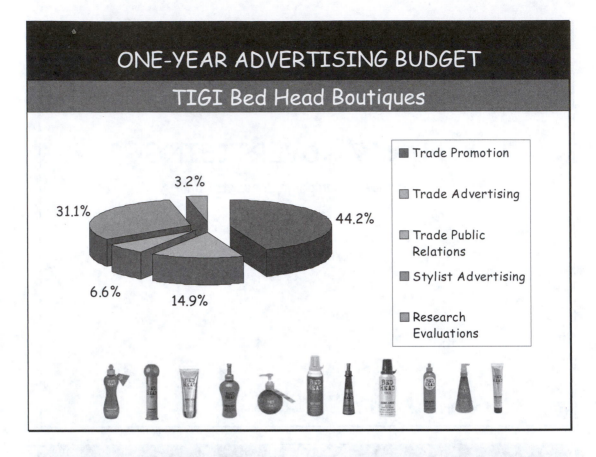

- Trade Promotion
- Trade Advertising
- Trade Public Relations
- Stylist Advertising
- Research Evaluations

3.2%
31.1%
44.2%
6.6%
14.9%

Problem One
Solving the Space Issue

TONI&GUY

BED HEAD®
TIGI BOUTIQUE

The New Bed Head Boutique

- Effective use of floor/shelf space
- Dynamic visual display
- Attractive to consumers

Problem Two

Solving the Image Issue

- Project Description
- Advertising Executions

Creative Strategy

Trade Print Ad

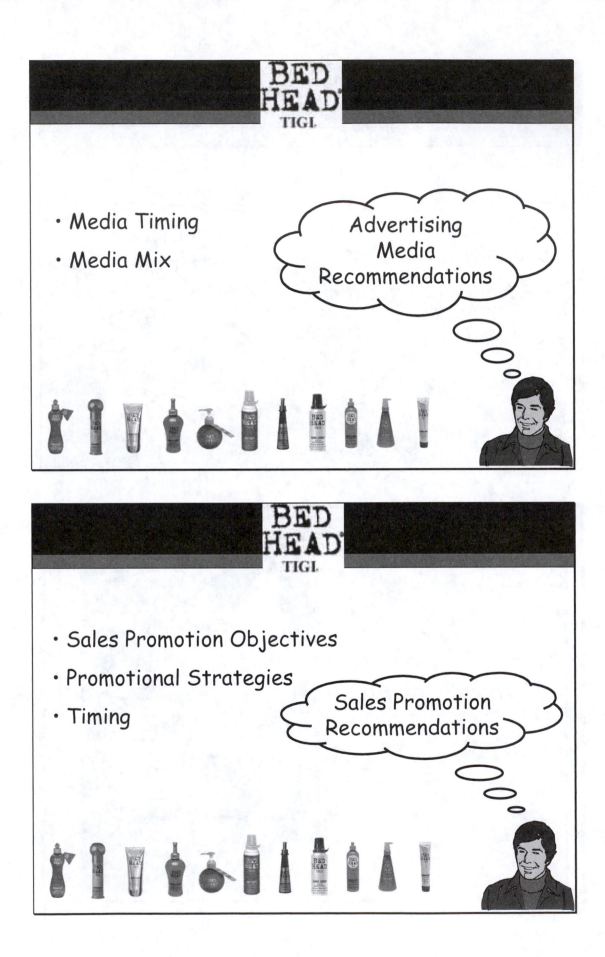

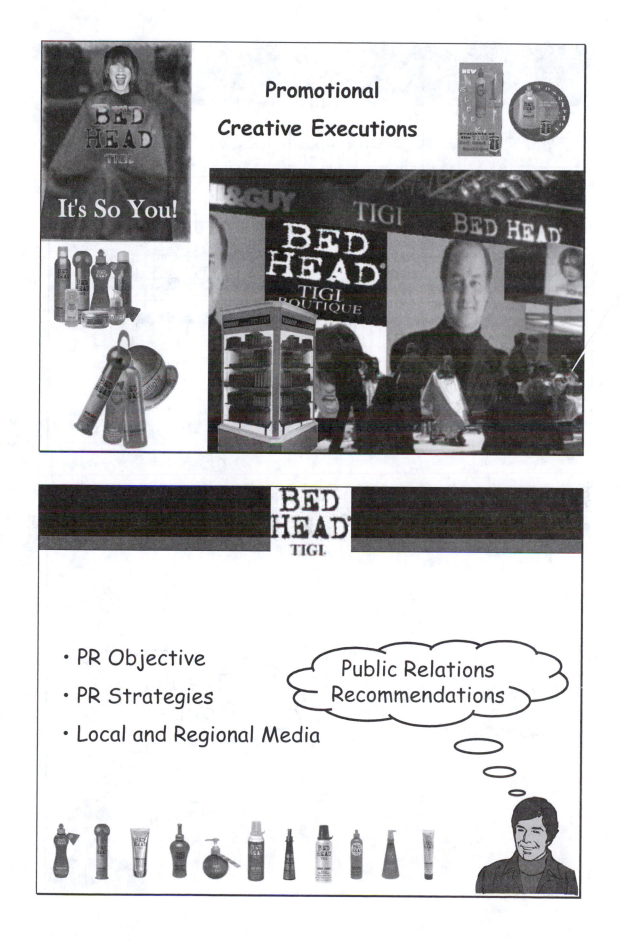

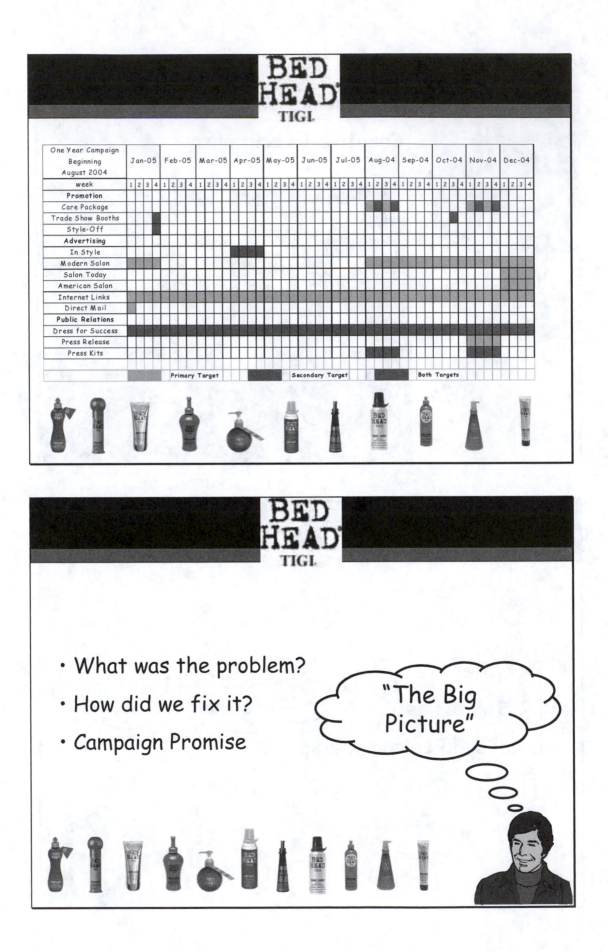